THE
UNDOING
OF
BABEL

Wilson, Wolfville

THE UNDOING OF BABEL

Watson Kirkconnell
The Man and His Work
edited by
J. R. C. Perkin

McClelland and Stewart Limited

Contents

Introduction

For more than fifty years the name of Watson Kirkconnell has been synonymous with linguistic ability, both in Canadian academic circles and farther afield. By the time he was thirty-three he had acquired competence in more than forty languages and his long career has developed this gift to the point where one may say that he has, in Douglas Bush's phrase, "nullified the curse of Babel."

To this monumental—one could probably say unique—achievement, Watson Kirkconnell has added major contributions as a teacher, scholar, administrator, and churchman, each aspect documented by the stream of publications which has flowed from his ready pen. Over the years honours and awards have naturally come his way, including honorary doctorates, chiefly in letters, from a dozen universities. As his eightieth birthday approached, Acadia University decided to mark that occasion by the publication of a volume of essays reflecting some of the dominant interests of his scholarship.

Selecting six areas of concentration was itself a difficult task because of the breadth of Watson Kirkconnell's skills and writings, but eventually a choice was made.

Milton studies have been one of Kirkconnell's abiding interests and since 1974 was the 300th anniversary of Milton's death it seemed appropriate to have one of the world's leading Milton scholars, Douglas Bush, writing on "Milton Three Hundred Years After."

Within the melting-pot of Canadian culture one important ingredient, particularly in the twentieth century, has been the Slavic element. Early in his teaching career Kirkconnell became proficient in the Slavic languages and taught many generations of students to share his enthusiasm. C. H. Andrusyshen was one such student; he later collaborated with his former teacher in two publications and contributes to this volume by an essay on "Canadian Ethnic Literary and Cultural Perspectives."

In 1945 and 1946 Watson Kirkconnell toured the francophone colleges and universities of Canada on behalf of the Humanities Research Council in company with Maurice Lebel, of Laval University. By virtue of his close friendship with Kirkconnell and his association with the Council, Dr. Lebel seemed the ideal person to write on the theme "Les Humanités dans l'enseignement supérieur au Canada."

Ever since the publication in 1928 of his *European Elegies*, Watson Kirkconnell has worked to enable anglophone readers to appreciate the beauty of literature originating in other languages. Another scholar who has attempted the difficult task of translating poetry is J. Max Patrick of the University of Wisconsin-Milwaukee, whose linguistic expertise is equal to the heavy technical demands of a chapter entitled "The Cleopatra Theme in World Literature up to 1700."

The late R. M. Wiles, office-mate of Kirkconnell for many years at McMaster University, had already begun work on an essay entitled "Research Methods in the Humanities" when we were saddened by the news of his sudden death early in 1974. Dr. E. Togo Salmon, also a colleague of McMaster days and currently President of the Humanities and Social Sciences Section of the Royal Society of Canada, graciously agreed to provide a paper at short notice and his topic, "The Changing Aspect of Clio," reflects the interest Kirkconnell has shown in classical history from undergraduate days.

One of the most demanding literary undertakings in which Watson Kirkconnell has been involved is the preparation, in collaboration with Mlle Jeannine Bélanger, of a diglott poetic version of the Psalter. Since one of my own special interests is translating for liturgical purposes my contribution to this volume deals with that theme.

I would like to record my thanks to the other writers for their willing and splendid co-operation; to the Governors of Acadia University for their support at every stage of this scheme; to

Dr. J. M. R. Beveridge, President of Acadia University, for his biographical chapter on his predecessor; to Mr. H. W. Ganong, Chief Librarian at Acadia University, for his patience and diligence in the formidable task of preparing a select bibliography of Dr. Kirkconnell's publications; and to Mrs. Anna Porter, Editorial Director of McClelland and Stewart Limited, for her advice and help at every stage from the initial suggestion to the publication of this book.

J. R. C. Perkin

Watson Kirkconnell:
A Biographical Sketch

by J. M. R. Beveridge,
Ph.D., M.D., F.R.S.C.

Watson Kirkconnell, one of our most distinguished Canadian scholars and certainly without peer as a linguist in our country, celebrates his eightieth birthday in 1975. On the initiative of Dr. J. R. C. Perkin, Head of the Department of Religious Studies, the Executive Committee of the Board of Governors warmly endorsed the proposal to sponsor the publication of a volume of essays to mark the occasion. Although it is an honour for me to be asked to write a brief biographical sketch for this volume, I do so with diffidence.

Dr. Kirkconnell is a fourth generation Canadian whose paternal great-grandparents came to Canada from Scotland in 1819 and his maternal great-grandparents (the Watsons) from Cumberland, England in that same year. The former settled in the Ottawa Valley and the latter near York (now Toronto). He was born in Port Hope, Ontario, on May 16th, 1895, the third of five children of Thomas Kirkconnell, headmaster of the local high school, and his wife, Bertha Watson. Because of indifferent health he did not attend school until the age of seven but once there quickly made up for lost time at least in terms of formal progress. One can well imagine that in any event the intellectual atmosphere of his home was such as to give him an excellent "head start." During his boyhood days he developed a great love for the woods and the fields and was completely happy in his frequent and often solitary excursions. He delighted in being alone in the woods and indulging, as he put it, in his "lone wolf propensity to study." From

11

these experiences alone in the woods one is inclined to conclude that he drew strength and inspiration as well as experiencing the first stirrings of a faith in the Divine.

In 1913 he entered Queen's University with first class honours in Mathematics, Physics, Chemistry, Biology, English, History, French, Latin, German, and Greek Literature. Although Mathematics was his best subject in high school, he proceeded to honours in Classics, maintaining a high academic record and graduating double medallist in Latin and Greek. He also received a Master of Arts degree in 1916.

Like so many young men of that time he enlisted in the army and after three years, confined to service on the home front because of his health, he was discharged with the rank of captain. Following a year and a half devoted to journalism and music, he was named Ontario's first I.O.D.E. overseas scholar and spent the academic year 1921-22 at Oxford University, where he showed his breadth and scope by earning the B.Litt. degree in Economics.

In September 1922 he was appointed as a lecturer in English at Wesley College (later known as United College and now as the University of Winnipeg) where he rose to the rank of full professor by 1933. That year he was made Head of the Department of Classics, a post he held until his move to McMaster University in 1940. At McMaster he reverted to the field of English, serving as Professor and Head of the Department. In 1948 he succeeded Dr. F. W. Patterson as President at Acadia University, serving until 1964. He continued his contributions to higher education, and to Acadia in particular, by teaching in the Department of English for four more years and from 1966 to 1968 he acted as Head of the Department.

Watson Kirkconnell was married to Isabel Peel in 1924 and in 1925 he suffered the tragic loss of his wife who died in giving birth to twin boys. For the next few years, he immersed himself in the prodigious work leading to the publication, in 1928, of *European Elegies*. He finally allowed his energies and thoughts to be diverted long enough to court and marry Hope Kitchener who bore him four children, of whom three daughters lived to maturity. All five of his children are teachers, two in colleges and three in schools.

Dr. Kirkconnell's great gift of achieving relatively quickly an excellent grasp and indeed a mastery of many foreign languages can only be explained by his great intellectual endowment, intense dedication, and complete commitment to learning. By 1930 he had

12

achieved a knowledge of fifty languages, and more than a passing acquaintance with many others.

His intellectual enthusiasms knew no bounds and his interests were indeed catholic. The years have not changed him in these respects. In addition to the areas of formal university study he showed a keen interest in such widely diverse fields as geology, anthropology, archaeology, music, nature studies, religious studies, and politics; in almost all these areas he has produced significant publications. If ever anyone deserves the appellation "polymath," it is he. In his own words, however, "my master passion has been the interpreting of foreign literatures in thousands of pages of my own verse translation. . . . " His scholarship has been enormously productive, resulting in the publication of over 170 books and brochures and of over 1,000 articles, as he has put it, "chiefly in the field of comparative literature."

Even after Dr. Kirkconnell became President of Acadia with the plethora of big and small problems characteristic of such a position, he continued his scholarly output and on occasion he substituted as a faculty member in English, Classics, and Economics. Very few men could have moved with such ease and authority in such widely different spheres of activity.

Dr. Kirkconnell's experience in education developed in him, as he put it, "a theory of pedagogy that called for a rigorous mastery in depth of two or three major disciplines, along with a 'vision of greatness' in arts, literature, science, and religion." It was of great importance, he thought, that in the arena of ideas, "the Christian faith should bear its witness." In the hope that exposure to a mature study of the English Bible would help many students to integrate an adult faith with teachings emanating from their secular studies, Dr. Kirkconnell succeeded in introducing a mandatory course in this subject for all arts sophomores.

Dr. Kirkconnell's awareness of God undoubtedly had its origins in his times of solitude when he wandered in the woods as a young boy; these were for him essentially religious experiences from which he derived and renewed his spiritual strength. His consciousness of the Divine was heightened by long religious instruction and at the age of twelve he became so spiritually aware that he was impelled to seek " . . . a right relationship with the God who was at once infinite Justice and infinite Love." He asked for and received baptism and church membership in the Port Hope Baptist Church. Thus began his commitment to Christianity which, although subjected to periods of doubt, sometimes perhaps even

13

approaching despair, survived and matured. Throughout his adult life he played an active and on many occasions a leading role in the Baptist denomination.

Dr. Kirkconnell's first participation in Baptist affairs was as a delegate from the First Church of Winnipeg to a special convention held in Calgary in 1924 to consider major matters of policy of the Baptist Union of Western Canada. In 1937 he was elected moderator of the Red River Valley Association and in 1938 was elected president of the Baptist Union of Western Canada for a term of two years.

In 1943 he was chairman of an All Canada Committee to plan for a nation-wide Baptist body and later he drafted a detailed constitution and proposed Act of federal incorporation. On the basis of hundreds of written suggestions, he modified extensively the proposal in 1944 and later on wrote a third and then a fourth and final draft which was accepted by all three regional conventions without amendment. He convened the first meeting of the council of the Baptist Federation of Canada on December 7, 1944.

In 1955, Dr. Kirkconnell attended the Golden Jubilee assembly of the Baptist World Alliance in London, England, where he addressed the Congress, eight thousand five hundred strong, on behalf of the five hundred delegates from the Baptist Federation of Canada.

His invaluable service on behalf of the Baptist denomination in Canada, coupled with his outstanding record as a scholar and a teacher, made it almost inevitable that he should be approached for the position of President of Acadia on the retirement of Dr. F. W. Patterson in 1948. Although he was its first lay president, he had been a leading figure in denominational activities for almost twenty years and could be expected to move easily and surely in Baptist circles. Despite his service in the Baptist cause he was subjected to harassments of one kind or another mostly from individuals or small groups within his own denomination. For the most part these criticisms and complaints scarcely merited a reply or a defence and were typical of the kind of pressure exerted by literal-minded members of denominational constituencies on the Presidents of church-controlled or related institutions. All these experiences, however, he bore with at least outward equanimity but it must have been difficult for him to keep his arsenal of words quiescent in the armoury. His pre-eminent qualification for the presidency, however, was that of a scholar of world-wide renown and because of this he brought to Acadia a further distinction to its existing well-deserved reputation.

14

In his own view, his chief claim to remembrance at the University was the initiative he took in persuading the executive heads of the six other post-secondary institutions to present a united front to the provincial government to gain a substantial measure of support for operating budgets on a regular basis—something that had obtained in most provinces in Canada for some time. It is certainly true that had not the government of the day listened to their plea, the parlous state of the Nova Scotian institutions would have worsened; there was already danger of the imminent and complete collapse of a number of them. Within two years the government established a University Grants Committee and since that time the level of support for operating budget has increased progressively.

In a more personal vein I should like to acknowledge the very helpful way in which Dr. Kirkconnell gave me a systematic briefing when I succeeded him in the office of president. The files had been reviewed and summaries appended to provide information in capsule form on all the matters of current importance. It was an invaluable service.

Dr. Kirkconnell's contributions to his field and to society in so many ways have been recognized by many honours, including a fellowship in the Royal Society of Canada, Coronation and Centennial medals, Medal of Service, Order of Canada, Humanities Research Council medal, and twelve honorary doctorates.

Dr. Kirkconnell is and has been throughout his life a man of high principle, dedicated to learning and to the advancement of understanding amongst all people. By his phenomenal gift for languages and by his great industry he has advanced the cause of civilization in our time in a way that few could have done. This book is a small acknowledgment of his great contribution.

Milton Three Hundred Years After

by Douglas Bush, Ph.D., F.B.A.

I t is a great pleasure to join in a tribute to Dr. Kirkconnell. To mention only two of his accomplishments, his unique services to Milton and Milton's readers were made possible (his Miltonic zeal being taken for granted) by his unique command of languages, which the rest of us, who rub along with three or four, must contemplate with envious despair. He might be said, in his individual capacity, to have nullified the curse of Babel.

The subject and title given to me seem to prescribe concentration on the present, and such an assignment is formidable enough to engender much diffidence; but Milton's present standing and the nature and direction of current scholarship and criticism cannot be even approached except in a large perspective. We may therefore as we go along remind ourselves, with unqualified brevity, of some attitudes of the past which have been more or less altered during the last half-century. A general premise is that Milton has fully shared in the general advance of modern criticism from loose impressionism to precise analysis of genres, form, ideas, language, imagery, rhythm, all the elements of poetry. A further premise is that, while there has been agreement on broad lines of modern reinterpretation, on many particular questions critics have naturally not shown the choric unanimity of Milton's angels singing around God's throne.

All of Milton's shorter poems as well as the longer ones have been more or less freshly studied, but we can look at only one, one which in recent decades has come to be regarded as the greatest middle-length poem in the language. *Lycidas* has not always had that status. We remember Dr. Johnson's unsparing condemnation and the reasons for it: his aversion to pastoralism and mythology and the mixing of such things with "the most awful and sacred truths" of religion, and also his neoclassical dislike of technical irregularities. During the nineteenth and the early twentieth centuries critics seem to have been generally dim in perception or inarticulate or both. *Lycidas* was, to be sure, called a masterpiece of classical art, but eulogy was commonly no less vague than short; and what had been seen as a crack in *Comus* was seen in *Lycidas* as a fatal split between the gracious young artist and the sour Puritan reformer. A line of well-known critics—Mark Pattison (1879), A. W. Verity, the editor of many texts, Oliver Elton, George Saintsbury, W. J. Courthope, Sir Walter Raleigh, Sir Herbert Grierson, and others—were in varying degrees unable to get far enough away from Dr. Johnson and their own anti-Puritanism to discern the theme of *Lycidas*: the dynamic inspiration of the poem appeared to be Milton's scorn for the clergy.

The only critic of the period I know of who really anticipated modern understanding was the poet William Vaughn Moody in his edition of Milton (1899). Moody recognized Milton's powerful re-creation of the pastoral mode and the thematic unity of a poem in which subtle and disciplined art barely controls surging emotion and wide-ranging symbolism; there is no split between the classicist poet and the Puritan, and the central inspiration is not the corrupt clergy but the "pathos of mortality" and unfulfilment. In 1915 John Bailey briefly stated the theme in a similar way. In 1924 Emile Legouis put Edward King aside to affirm that the subject of *Lycidas* was Milton himself: hence the force and passion which even impercipient critics had felt, though they had mistaken the cause. In the first edition (1926) of what was to be a long-lived handbook, J. H. Hanford carried on the idea of Milton's personal and deeply religious consciousness of the blighting of high promise by early death.

This view was elaborated in E. M. W. Tillyard's *Milton* (1930): the real subject is Milton, not King, but Milton's apprehension of death is not the whole. Tillyard's outline of the structure showed how, through the several sections and their limited climaxes, the poet in the final crescendo achieves the only satisfying consolation, that "The loss or possible loss of human fame is made good by fame in heaven." Such a summary oversimplifies both the interpretation and the poem, but it indicates arrival at a valid grasp of the true theme and greatness of *Lycidas*. Although some eminent older critics continued to play the old tune, during the past forty-five years criticism has reached new levels of insight. The main grounds of Dr. Johnson's complaints have become the main grounds for analysis of Milton's powerful and subtle re-creation of a genre, of a tragic theme at once deeply personal and greatly impersonal, of an intense spiritual struggle finally resolved by a beatific vision.

Milton's sonnets, whatever their manifold interest, might seem to offer little room for opposed views; yet, if we could go into continuing scholarly debates, debates which involve both bio-graphical and interpretative problems, we should have to take account of the early "How soon hath time" and the later "When I consider how my light is spent" and "Methought I saw my late espoused saint." The last two have inspired what some or many may think strange aberrations. To speak only of the last one, it has been argued that the espoused saint was the poet's first wife, not his second; that she was neither wife but a purely ideal woman; and that the sonnet is an abstract parable of salvation.

The sonnets were, of course, only occasional utterances during the long period Milton gave mainly to prose. The historical back-ground, foreground, and substance of his thinking, for the most part solidly set forth by Masson, have been enlarged or modified in many special studies and conspicuously in the *Complete Prose Works* being edited by Don M. Wolfe and his associates. Impor-tant pioneers in the modern analysis of Milton's political and reli-gious thought, especially his great principle of "Christian Lib-erty," were the Canadian Arthur Woodhouse, Arthur Barker, and Ernest Sirluck: they did much to show how Milton, facing the difficult problems of freedom and authority, came to unite fervent liberal Puritanism with classical republicanism. In this complex area such modern inquiry has achieved more fully informed, more precise, and more discriminating elucidation than Masson's of Milton's evolving convictions, aims, and methods, and of his his-torical and contemporary affinities and antagonisms, but it has not made, indeed could not make, a radical change in the broad estab-lished view of his crusade for liberty, disciplined liberty, on all fronts.

In Milton's purely theological thought, however, a radical change of definition and interpretation has been strongly urged. From the first publication and translation of his large treatise, *De Doctrina Christiana* (1825), critics saw Milton as a follower of the

19

Arian heresy, the doctrine which denied a consubstantial, coequal, and coeternal Trinity and conceived the Son as a being created out of nothing by the Father and hence in nature and function far inferior to the Son of orthodox Christianity. The chief modern exponent of the Arian or anti-Trinitarian Milton has been Maurice Kelley (*This Great Argument*, 1941; various articles; the commentary in the latest volume of the *Complete Prose Works*, 1973). That traditional view has of late years been challenged by several scholars, W. B. Hunter, C. A. Patrides, and J. H. Adamson, who arrived independently at approximately similar positions: that Milton did not see himself as an Arian and was not one, but was in accord with early Fathers' "subordinationist" doctrine, a doctrine revived by Milton's contemporaries, such as Ralph Cudworth, the Cambridge Platonist. (These scholars' articles, revised, are collected in *Bright Essence*, 1971.) As Miltonists are well aware, this question is especially significant for our reading of *Paradise Lost*; they are also well aware that the theology of the poem differs on various points from that of the treatise. The new interpretation gives the Son a divine nature and power which make Him "of fundamental importance in the act of creation, the revelation of the Godhead within history, and the salvation of man" (*Bright Essence*, vii).

Milton would have been one of the great poets even if he had never composed *Paradise Lost*, but during its three hundred years of existence that epic has naturally been the chief determinant of its author's general poetic character and reputation. We may therefore briefly recall successive phases of critical history, however commonplace these data are. In the early eighteenth century, when the poem was already a classic, the representative and very laudatory Addison applied the literary standards of neoclassical orthodoxy. Those mainly external criteria in some degree gave way to the more individual and vital judgment of a great critic, Dr. Johnson. The romantic age brought in new criteria, and two of the poets, thoroughly hostile to orthodox Christianity, in a few sentences launched a conception of the poem and the poet which has survived into our own time. The revolutionary Blake and Shelley, making over Milton in their own image, saw him as a great rebel who was of the devil's party without knowing it and who projected his rebellious self into Satan. To jump down to the present, the vehemently anti-Christian William Empson applauds "the manly and appreciative attitude of Blake and Shelley, who said that the reason why the poem is so good is that it makes God so bad." This dogma and the degree of acceptance it has had are very curious: none of the "Satanists" would ever have said that Shakespeare projected himself into Richard III or Iago or Macbeth or would have taken those great villains as their interpretative guides to the several plays. One cannot leave the romantic age without quoting those familiar words of Coleridge which contain a sufficient answer to Satanism:

> He was, as every truly great poet has ever been, a good man; but finding it impossible to realize his own aspirations, either in religion or politics, or society, he gave up his heart to the living spirit and light within him, and avenged himself on the world by enriching it with this record of his own transcendent ideal.

Another view, also born in the romantic age, seems to have become predominant in the Victorian; one representative, unhappily, was Matthew Arnold. In this view the poet, although he had turned into a grim, even repellent, Puritan, was still somehow endowed with a sublime organ voice; hence his beliefs and ideas must be dismissed and *Paradise Lost* be enjoyed for its aesthetic beauties, the incomparable artistry of its grand style and rhythm. This attitude was crystallized in 1900 in Sir Walter Raleigh's notorious dictum that "The *Paradise Lost* is not the less an eternal monument because it is a monument to dead ideas."

While specifically Puritan doctrines and ideals are almost invisible in *Paradise Lost*, the Puritan tradition has been, or was until recent times, more congenial to Americans than to Englishmen, and it was quite logical that, from about 1917 onward, several American scholars, especially the late J. H. Hanford, should quietly carry on a revisionist movement. These scholars, with much fuller comprehension than most of their predecessors of Milton and his literary and ideological background and inheritance, by degrees erased the stereotype of the harsh Puritan with his sublime gift and established a new and unified image of the liberal Christian humanist of the Renaissance. Milton's prose and poetry were seen as the expression of active and important beliefs and principles, as an individual but coherent blend of classical and Renaissance reason and culture with Reformation Protestantism. This radical rehabilitation of Milton was largely confined to a small but growing tribe of academic specialists. A wider impact was made in 1925 and 1930 by the books of Saurat and Tillyard, which, if not wholly emancipated from the old image, did in the main present the new Milton, a human, humane, and passionate man, thinker, and poet.

Meanwhile, among the literary intelligentsia another kind of impact was being made by the explosive buckshot of Ezra Pound and the quieter sniping of T. S. Eliot and others. Whereas the Victorians were inclined to dismiss the Puritan reformer and supposed fundamentalist in order to save and exalt the supreme artist, these new attacks were aimed at the artist as well. Poets seeking to inaugurate a poetic revolution felt the need of destroying the authority of the Miltonic tradition. Thus in 1933 F. R. Leavis could make a declaration which was to become as notorious as Raleigh's: "Milton's dislodgment, in the past decade, after his two centuries of predominance, was effected with remarkably little fuss." Donne was seated on the now vacant throne; he and Marvell, as more or less "metaphysical" poets, were the older English masters nearest to the aims and methods of the new poetry. And the new creed and hierarchy got strong support from the so-called New Critics.

In regard to Milton's alleged dislodgment, we might for a moment descend to some statistics (derived from the standard bibliographies and including editions and translations but not reviews). In 1933, the year of Dr. Leavis' wishful assertion, Donne gave birth to three books and three articles, Milton to twelve books and twenty-eight articles. It might of course be said that academic scholars and critics lagged behind the *literati*, but it was mainly academic people who wrote about Donne. As for the prodigious growth of what came to be called the Milton industry, one set of figures is enough: the year 1920 yielded six books and sixteen articles; half a century later, in 1970, there were twenty-one books, a hundred and ten articles, and nineteen dissertations. One general reason for this great increase was the great increase in the number of academic scholars and critics who were at work in all areas of literature. But this army might have deserted Milton for other gods and it did not; he has continued to attract a larger number of critics than probably any author except Shakespeare. Such statistics are, to be sure, a very crude weathervane, but they have some significance.

To return to *Paradise Lost*, interpretation of the poem received much fresh stimulus in the 1940's, positive from C. S. Lewis, B. Rajan, and others, negative from A. J. A. Waldock and his supporters. Waldock, treating a richly symbolic epic as if it were a realistic novel, pounced on unrealistic inconsistencies; he also

22

showed an inability to understand religious and ethical values. His perversely acute case for the prosecution helped greatly to evoke the best defence, illuminating studies from soundly acute critics now, happily, far too numerous to name. These interpreters, whatever their personal creeds, have had the prime virtue of informed and imaginative sympathy with Milton's theme, with his passionate and much-tried faith in God's providence and in man's freedom and responsibility. Further, the qualities the New Critics had exploited in Donne and his fellows, "wit," irony, ambiguity, paradox, these and other supposedly unMiltonic qualities have been found to be active, below the smooth surface, in *Paradise Lost*. The close reading and insight of these many critics have enormously enriched our sense of the vitality and functional complexity of Milton's language and of his imaginative and emotional engagement.

In *Lycidas*, the threatening thought of early death had compelled the young poet to take stock of his faith in Providence, and, after anguished struggle, that faith emerged triumphant, not through argument but through a vision of heavenly fulfilment. Thirty years later, after Milton had lost all confidence in the mass of men of the past and present, the old question—which had been carried on in his prose works—was renewed in the major poems, poems composed in a time of political reaction and growing rationalistic scepticism. In our time, *Paradise Lost* has been read freshly as a grand Christian myth of the human situation, of man's whole history and destiny, the everlasting plight of the fallen world. The poet would have shared the view summed up with unMiltonic levity in a presumably modern limerick:

> Man made a happy beginning,
> But spoiled his chances by sinning.
> We hope that the story
> May end to God's glory,
> But at present the other side's winning.

We may look briefly at some parts or aspects of the poem which in past or recent times have more or less hindered readers' receptivity. It is a critical commonplace, as Stanley Fish has said in reaffirming it, that "the central issue in Milton's poetry is the relationship between man and God." Throughout *Paradise Lost* we should see and feel that man's fall was not in Milton's mind a single remote event but an experience continually reenacted, that heaven and hell and paradisal Eden are not merely places but

23

existential states of mind. One of the services of modern criticism has been the rehabilitation of the last books of *Paradise Lost*, books so often condemned as a dead weight by some modern along with earlier critics. Using the epic convention of prophecy, Milton was able to give an historical preview of the waste land of the world that Adam and Eve were about to enter. Yet his realistic survey of that dark history, dark even in the Christian era, could not overcome his belief in the capacity of the individual sinner, through penitence, earnest effort, and divine grace, to achieve a paradise within far happier than the lost Eden.

No doubt we can share the poet's vision of evil and tragic loss much more readily than his unshakable belief in the possibility of regeneration and in the Providential plan which makes the poem a divine comedy, a tragedy with a far-off happy ending when "God shall be all in all." However remote Milton's religious beliefs may be from most modern readers, they should be able to respond at least to his picture of the everlasting war between good and evil in the mind and heart of man and hence in the world at large. But we must not try to make *Paradise Lost* "relevant" by ignoring the other half of Milton's vision; it is a prime necessity that we read him—or any author of the past—on his own terms, in this case traditional Christian terms. Whatever else we incline to do, we must submit our minds to his, not his to ours; the latter process is exemplified by some modern directors' treatment of Shakespeare.

A main stumbling block for many readers has been Milton's supposed conception and presentation of God as an arbitrary tyrant, an almighty cat playing with a doomed pair of mice. That large problem cannot be disposed of in a paragraph, but some lines taken by modern criticism can be suggested: that Milton fervently denied Calvinistic predestination and fervently asserted man's free will, since freedom must include freedom to sin; that God is, among other things, the source and symbol of moral law, which can be apprehended by man, who has the divine endowment of right reason, however impaired in a fallen world; that, because God does stand for supreme law, his utterances must have the unadorned austerity of naked truth; and that, for the sake of celestial drama in an heroic poem of traditional concreteness, the voice of law and justice and the Son's mild voice of love and mercy may seem to be opposed, but in fact are in accord, since God anticipates or approves the attitudes of the Son toward erring man. Their combined attributes are simply the attributes of Deity.

The real tyrant is, of course, not God but Satan. Nowadays we see, as one of the most pervasive and potent elements in the poem, the play of dramatic irony, based as always on the audience's knowledge of the outcome in contrast with the blindness of the actors. Hence the words and actions of both Satan and his fellows and Adam and Eve carry either hostile or compassionate irony, and that puts the reader's discernment to a continual test, since he too is fallen and may be disposed to share the wrong feelings of the human pair or even of Satan. There is the ironic fact that the tremendous Satan has the qualities of leadership associated with the traditional epic hero, although nearly everything he says and does reveals his corruption. One important exception, the soliloquy he utters when he reaches the earth, shows the working of conscience and thereby gives him a new dimension, a tragic potentiality which, however, is not to be realized. And along with irony goes a related and very significant strain of parody. Satan, God's would-be conqueror, is a pseudo-God. The intermittent allegory of Sin and Death (derived from James 1:15), which was censured by Addison and Dr. Johnson as a breach of decorum, has been recognized as one of Milton's most effective inventions. Satan and his incestuous paramour and offspring are a monstrous parody of the Trinity, an idea notably concentrated in Sin's looking forward to Satan's triumph, when "I shall reign / At thy right hand voluptuous." So too hell is a parody of heaven. In the grand infernal debate Mammon, holding out the promise of gold and gems in their desert soil, declares: "Nor want we skill or art, from whence to raise / Magnificence; and what can heav'n show more?" Both these items illustrate Milton's continual use of parallel and contrast. This principle of organization, long recognized in a limited degree, has been much more fully and minutely extended, so that the poem has become a more and more complex and coherent network of both girders and filaments, literal and symbolic.

Along with scholarly knowledge of Milton's place in the pattern of seventeenth-century religion, philosophy, politics, and science, the new tribe of critics has displayed sensitive and precise aesthetic perceptiveness in all areas. They have shown how far conventional complaints about Milton's generalizing language and style came from sheer incapacity for reading him: *Paradise Lost*, in its verbal texture as well as in its total design, is rich in subtle implication and suggestion. The grand style which Dr. Leavis and others pronounced heavy rhetoric is, in fact, an instrument of infinite flexibility. The amount of Latinate language has been shown to be greatly exaggerated and the poet's use of it to be as expressive as his simplicity. The second of the quotations just above is a signal example of Milton's inspired use of an abstract Latinate word, "Magnificence." In the first quotation the word "voluptuous" gives its shock by being retarded as it might be in Latin verse; the item reminds us that another means of expressive force is freely dislocated word-order and syntax, though the sense is never unclear—as it so often is in the "English" Shakespeare. As for Milton's command of rhythm, which is always inseparable from his meaning and emotional charge, Dr. Leavis heard only deadly monotony; T. S. Eliot, whatever his early hostility on other grounds, affirmed that Milton "is never monotonous." Since Eliot was himself a master of expressive rhythm and since Dr. Leavis' prose suggests no very sensitive ear, we have a choice of oracles. More concrete evidence is supplied by our own experience and the critical analyses of modern experts in metrics.

On the whole it can be said that many traditional or modern complaints have been pretty thoroughly demolished, and that modern criticism operates on a plane of general agreement about the immense vitality and complexity of the poem, whatever central or marginal questions remain in debate. Our trouble nowadays is not, as it used to be, "darkness visible"; instead, perhaps, our minds are sometimes "Dark with excessive bright." The critical spectrum was closely scrutinized by Irene Samuel in 1968: a challenging point of her own was that *Paradise Lost* is rather a *paideia* than a theodicy. The necessary brevity of this glance at the poem may warrant taking refuge in the contrast between two generalities, one of them Dr. Leavis' assertion of 1933, the other Frank Kermode's saying of 1957, that the time was not far off when *Paradise Lost* would be read once more "as the most perfect achievement of English poetry, perhaps the richest and most intricately beautiful poem in the world."

Disparagement of *Paradise Regained* in comparison with its predecessor began in Milton's lifetime and greatly vexed him, and it has continued down to our time. Many readers have seen a coldly rational moral debate which lacks the imaginative magnitude and splendour of *Paradise Lost*. Decorum does put Milton's sensuous instincts under austere restraint, but not his moral and religious passion. Most traditional complaints have been nullified by the full realization that the "brief epic," while a logical and predestined sequel to *Paradise Lost*, is much more openly a *pai-*

26

deia and must be read as an altogether different kind of poem. Modern critics have recognized subtle and mounting dramatic tension in Satan's efforts to discover Christ's true nature, identity, and mission, and the young hero's own progressive discovery of the answers. The drama moves from the temptation to distrust God's providence through the rising scale of the various seductive allurements of worldy action and power. It ends with a spectacular return to distrust of God's providence, with the protagonist's becoming conscious of his divine Sonship, and with his adversary's fall. Critics have found further complexity and density in regard to typology, Christ's triple offices of prophet, priest, and king, his maintenance of the "kingdom" of his church, and Milton's response to millenarianism. Yet it may still be right to see his prime broad purpose in the presentation of the second Adam as the earthly complement of the exalted Son of *Paradise Lost*, as the perfect exemplar of the Christian knowledge, patient fortitude, and obedient humility of which the first Adam learned when he was leaving Eden. The poem is the disillusioned Christian revolutionist's most direct statement of the possibility of true heroism and salvation that is still open to individual man.

Samson Agonistes is—if we remain unconvinced by some modern arguments for an early date—Milton's last treatment of the theme of temptation and resistance which he had variously bodied forth in *Comus, Lycidas*, and the two epics. In this psychological drama, the hero's chief temptation is yielding to despair, to the conviction that he has forfeited God's favour and support. While it has been said that a Christian cannot write a tragedy, it is clear that Milton was a Christian and that *Samson* is a tragedy, even in spirit a Christian tragedy, although it is kept so strictly within the Hebrew frame that no specifically Christian idea is admitted, not even that of immortality. As Arthur Woodhouse said, trust in God's providence as the long-range, ultimate determinant does not preclude tragic experience for the limited human understanding.

In the typological tradition, Samson was one of the "types" of Christ, and critics see a rather special kind of typology here. Samson is both like and unlike the Christ of *Paradise Regained*; he is, like Adam, a sinner, but he cannot, like Adam, become a Christian before Christ. He is obviously far from the mere brawny Hercules of the book of Judges. In both structure and texture, the drama is packed with Sophoclean irony and ambiguity (which begin with the title and first line), and the protagonist is Sophoclean in that his will is subjected to a series of tests or temptations.

27

In orthodox modern interpretation, Samson rises from wounded pride and despair to religious penitence, humility, and confidence in a renewed relationship with God which makes his physical fate of no account. This view of regeneration, which modern criticism has elaborated, finds its support in Milton's lifelong concern with the way of righteousness and salvation and in a general kinship with the epics. It has had at least one forceful opponent: Irene Samuel, starting from Samson's ruthless destruction of the Philistines, argues that he is less a sanctified martyr than an Aristotelian hero who, despite his virtues, is destroyed by a *hamartia*, a *hubris*, more radical than Agamemnon's.[1] One may mention an idea, prominent in the older modern criticism, which the newer generation of critics seems inclined to pass by as presumably invalid or irrelevant: that, although the drama is wholly objective and impersonal, its impassioned strength owes something to the author's feeling a partial parallel between himself and his hero, "Eyeless in Gaza at the mill with slaves." At any rate, for those readers who cannot enter fully into the two epics, and perhaps even for some who can, *Samson* may be Milton's most completely "relevant" and moving work.

As for Milton in general, the army of scholar-critics would agree that, while many matters of fact or opinion remain debatable, the last half-century has achieved a breadth and depth of enlightenment hardly approached before; and it may be assumed that that essential effort will continue. Yet some queries may arise. Contemplating the huge amount of criticism, we may wonder whether the most zealous student has of late years been able to keep track of it —much less to enlarge his education in other areas. Criticism must grow, like ballads, by incremental repetition; but there can be more repetition than increment, at least valuable increment. Of course all literary discussion in recent times has risked encountering the law of diminishing returns, but the more eminent the author the more formidable are the coral reefs of commentary that build up around him.

In addition to sheer overwhelming quantity and much unevenness of quality, one might note the emergence of two specific diseases (the last word would be denounced in some quarters). Without denying the sexual element in Milton's poetic vision, one may object to automatic, undiscriminating Freudianism. Since for the Freudian critic all images the outer and inner worlds afford are sexual, he has unlimited scope with Milton as with other authors, and fantasies commonly soar or sink far beyond any level of rationality or relevance. The newer and still more infectious cult of numerology has likewise unlimited horizons: traditional support can be found for a variety of meanings symbolized by any one number, so that the eager customer in the mystical supermarket can always find one that suits his fancy. Since Milton gave no hint of any concern with numerology, the critic is free to follow the method of the man in *Pickwick Papers* who wrote on Chinese metaphysics by reading an encyclopaedia article on China and another on metaphysics and combining them. We can readily imagine what the poet would say about such obfuscation of his earnest messages to mankind. It may be more than a coincidence that these modes of freakishness have developed during a time in which classical education, a traditional nurse of common sense, has suffered a conspicuous decline.

Having registered these general and special misgivings—the misgivings of an old fogey who can't keep up with the march of mind—I may repeat that, in the main, modern scholarship and criticism have brought a far richer understanding of Milton the man, the thinker, the crusader, and the poet than was ever formerly possible for anyone except a superhumanly ideal reader of the seventeenth century. In that achievement, study of the history of ideas and acute aesthetic perception have both played a notable part. But one may raise a last, large question. Does the immense and mainly fruitful writing of specialists in the past half-century mean that Milton is being read correspondingly more by that very limited body of non-academic people who read poetry? From casual talk with other teachers I know that my experience in teaching Milton for thirty-odd years was quite typical: that is, that three-fourths or more of the undergraduates did genuinely enjoy him and gave authentic evidence of more or less warm and sensitive responsiveness. But at my back I always hear, as others do, the question whether such students ever return to Milton (or to other great writers of the past) after they leave college. The pollsters have not got around to that question. If the humanities are to extend, or even to retain, what we at least believe is their saving power in a world whose deeper troubles may not be cured by social scientists and computers, they must be kept humane; and critics, along with their search for new light, must surely do more to reach the mass of educated people and not write only for one another. We must surely accept what Professor Kermode has called the "basic humanistic job" of the university, "to perpetuate the literary public," even though, thinking of the present world and the common indifference or hostility toward the past, we may confess—to echo Ernest Bramah's Kai Lung—that our "hopes of the future are concave in the extreme."

Note

1 "*Samson Agonistes* as Tragedy," *Calm of Mind*, J. A. Wittreich, ed. (Cleveland and London, 1971). This collection of new essays is almost wholly devoted to *Paradise Regained* and *Samson*. These works are also the subjects of the essays in *The Prison and the Pinnacle*, B. Rajan, ed. (Toronto and London, 1973).

I may cite a forthcoming book by Edward Le Comte which contains a full defence of the traditional dating of *Samson* and also remarks on the parallel between Milton's situation and his hero's.

Canadian Ethnic Literary and Cultural Perspectives

by C. H. Andrusyshen, Ph.D., F.R.S.C.

A new term in Canadian multiculturalism has recently come into being, viz., *vertical mosaic*, which was invented by Professor John Porter who, in his book bearing that very title, attempts to prove that the two chief national groups in Canada, Anglo-Saxon and French, seek to prevent their fellow-Canadians of other ethnic extractions from achieving authoritative positions in this country. While it is true that many New Canadians are to be found in various governmental posts, their urge to elevate themselves to higher public offices, in actual governing bodies, meets with a firm refusal on the part of the two predominant segments of our national society. To the ethnic elements who seem to be treated so unequally, this smacks of discrimination. For that reason most of the still so-called "foreign" masses, feeling themselves somewhat slighted, do not participate fully in national matters, at least not to the extent they might. To be sure, they do not, on that account, form any kind of ghettoes, but their disappointment at being scanted in high places does not increase their enthusiasm for the tasks which should be considered of mutual concern to Canadians as a whole. Whether rightly or wrongly, certain, but not all, ethnic groups which believe themselves to be pushed aside by the two ruling classes, continue mainly to foster their particular cultures, in the process of which they tend well-nigh to forget that they should likewise work for Canada's improvement in cultivating all the fields of its endeavour in order to help it become a nation second to none. The New Canadians certainly remain a

31

solid part of the Canadian mosaic; however, much to their disenchantment, only vertically so; horizontally, they are limited to much lower levels.

On one occasion, it is said, the former prime minister of Canada, W. L. Mackenzie King, stated quite rightly that there are many nations with too much history, whereas Canada has too much geography. With geography, of course, goes demography; and, in the country over which he presided, the ethnic groups were then beginning to play quite an important role. Among them the Slavs, who, after the Anglo-Canadians, the French, and the Germans, form the fourth largest section of the population, are to be considered ethnographically more significant than even the two founding races, since upon their arrival here they brought with them the very roots of their folklore which they implanted in the new soil, tending them until they stemmed and spread into a variegated profusion to be marvelled at. The Anglo-Saxons and the French, on the other hand, began their existence on this side of the Atlantic from the upper strata and higher echelons. As genuine tillers of the land, those who immigrated to Canada from central and eastern Europe, at the very beginning possessed such human ideals which the discoverers of this part of the world in certain measure lacked. The latter were mostly traders engaged in business matters which, in a way, did not make them inclined to treat religious and spiritual issues to the fullest extent. This general statement may appear to be an exaggeration, for both the English and French elements, especially the latter, were not devoid of definite spiritual symptoms. What is really meant in this case is that the New Canadians, finding themselves in what, to them, was a foreign region and a wilderness, felt a greater need of divine assistance and exerted a greater endeavour to cultivate it by a more intense piety.

It soon became evident that if the English-speaking population were to understand their fellow-Canadians of other national backgrounds, many such works as John Murray Gibbon's *Canadian Mosaic: the Making of a Northern Nation* were needed, and more translations of their lyrics, poems, ballads into English were necessary to acquaint the predominant English race with the religious and secular manners and customs of those aliens who began to appear among them in ever increasing numbers. These informative materials were difficult to find, as no newcomers to Canada as yet knew English well enough to produce at least a tolerable translation of their native or New Canadian writers' works. Not until Dr.

Watson Kirkconnell, while still in Winnipeg, Manitoba, became interested in as many ethnic groups as he could was the mutual acquaintanceship between the English Canadians and the newcomers made possible. No better linguist was to be found for this purpose. The acme of his endeavour in the thirties was his translation and publication of a limited number of poems and lyrics by certain representatives of seven ethnic bodies, entitled *Canadian Overtones*, published in Winnipeg in 1937. In it Dr. Kirkconnell presented the mentality of the peoples whose languages he began to study precisely for the purpose of rendering their writings understandable to the Canadians of his race, as well as to those of other respective races who had already learned to read the chief language of this country.

His short but most important introduction to this brief paperback is plainly outspoken indeed. In it, as tactfully as he could, he castigated his compatriots for considering the New Canadians as menial races incapable of intellectual development and fit only to serve their masters. It was mostly through his efforts that this snobbish attitude towards the immigrants later changed into a mood of acceptance on the part of the as yet unfriendly Anglo-Saxon element, particularly when the former's colourful ethnography was made evident to the Canadians as a whole. Such individuals as Florence Randal Livesay, Percival Cundy, A. J. Hunter, with Watson Kirkconnell and a few others, detected the true worth in the poetry that these colonizing types produced, and revealed them to all Canadians as sedulous in thinking lofty thoughts.

Furthermore, in his introduction to this anthology, Dr. Kirkconnell expressed his fears that, while burdened by scorn and derision, the future generations of these pioneers might eventually forswear their ancestral heritage. Such deserters he ranked as narrow, shallow men, for, in his opinion, they should have striven to gainsay "the ignorant assumption of many an English citizen that alien origin is a natural mark of inferiority." Being a well-rounded intellectual, of the Renaissance category, Dr. Kirkconnell was the foremost Canadian who in the thirties of the present century succeeded in effecting the beginnings of mutual concord between his own national kind and those who sought refuge in Canada from the miseries they suffered in central and eastern Europe.

As mentioned above, he lost no time in pursuing this success by delving into the poetic expression of those so-styled peculiar people. Almost in every case their earliest poetry, written in Canada,

33

dealt with the pains and sorrows they experienced in the new land which to them, especially in the prairie provinces, was a wilderness or a barrenness which they were destined to transform into a land flowing with milk and honey. Much of their poetry, particularly that written by Ukrainians, was rendered in a pessimistic tone for quite some time. Icelandic poetry, judging by the selections translated in the *Overtones*, appears to be more optimistic and of a higher degree of intellectuality than the rest of the material included in this volume. If one were to ask for the reason for these qualities, the answer would lie in the fact that the Icelanders hardly endured the same yoke of servitude in their native land as did the Slavs in theirs. Although the Icelanders were somewhat detached and isolated from Europe, nevertheless, for almost a millenium, they belonged to the Scandinavian culture and were brought up on Old Norse sagas and Eddas. These continued to some degree to be cultivated by the imaginative spirit of this people who came here in the seventies of the past century when they first settled in Nova Scotia and southern Ontario until, by force of unfavourable circumstances in those regions, they moved westward and established themselves in Winnipeg and Gimli, Manitoba, with a smaller number of them going as far as southern Alberta.

While teaching in Wesley College (now the University of Winnipeg), Watson Kirkconnell found himself surrounded by Icelanders whose language was taught there. It was perhaps their influence that made him seek connections with other ethnic groups in Manitoba. But for a long period yet his enthusiasm was concentrated mainly on what was produced in Icelandic in Canada. To such an extent did his zeal for their poetry increase that he compared some of the poets he selected to certain Anglo-Canadian poets of the time, and Stephan G. Stephansson (1853-1927) he considered as equal to and, in certain respects, surpassing such a pre-eminent poet as E. J. Pratt. His poems, descriptive of nature, viz., "Spruce Forest," and those in which he recorded his personal experiences in Western Canada, are philosophic in scope and soaring with impressionism, as are many poems and lyrics of the other fifteen bards, especially those of Sigurður Júlíus Jóhannesson, particularly in his lyrical verses "What Art Thou Life?" and "To a Mouse in a Trap."

To what extent the translator elaborated upon the originals to sound so excellently in English one has no way of knowing. It has been argued, for example, that the Russian Romantic poet V. A. Zhukovsky translated Gray's "Elegy Written in a Country

34

Churchyard" so matchlessly that it sounds much better in Russian than in English. Was this likewise the case of Kirkconnell with regard to the Icelandic poets of his predilection? The answer to this question, however, would be a mere supposition, for most of the Icelandic poets he dealt with were acute in intelligence (no reflections on Gray intended!) and highly capable of producing first-rank poetry which could hardly be excelled by any translator. And yet, in the estimation of many, Watson Kirkconnell is one of the greatest Canadian poets, painstaking enough to be compared to Zhukovsky.

In his opinion, Swedish-Canadian poetry, represented by three modern skalds, as well as that of a single Norwegian one, in this collection, is just as lofty in scale. It is only too evident that they not only inherited the literary traditions of their respective countries but were likewise influenced by Western European recent trends in fine letters.

Hungarians, who are neither Slavs nor Scandinavians but Ugro-Finnish in origin, have also evolved a large number of poets, most of them well-schooled in their native land. Only three appear in *Canadian Overtones*, but these are quite representative of their country's prosodic assets. They may well be compared to the Ukrainian versifiers, for they, too, express their nostalgic pensiveness as they poetize their feelings in the new land, which they intermingle with the sentimentality of their connection with their native country. This is particularly the case of Charlotte Petényi, the wife of a former Hungarian consul in Winnipeg, who, in her "Christmas in Canada," seems to evoke her joy through her tears. Another woman, Rózsa Páll Kovács, who wrote in the first decade of this century, voices her emotion very poignantly in her "Non-Preferred" which reflects what Kirkconnell calls "the callousness of immigration laws." In her other poem, "West-Bound," she artistically describes the Canadian wilderness seen from the train window before she reaches Winnipeg, "the island of promise."

It is fairly valid to state that the two principal "nations" in Canada do not now mind if other ethnic groups develop their respective cultures in their midst. Nevertheless, it is likewise true that the existence of these groups, which are activated by their innate ethnographical processes, would not be so obvious as to create a third frictional segment of Canadian population quite distinct from the two-nation concept of the Canadian compound. All contrary matters aside, it is becoming somewhat evident that the

35

Canadian government, despite its multicultural policy, would like to be less concerned with the third ethnic element within its boundaries. If it has not as yet expressed itself firmly to that effect, the reason is probably that, for political motives, it does not want to antagonize the already clamouring third of its inhabitants. In fact, the English authorities of this land would like to see these groups integrated into Anglo-Saxonism as soon as possible. To an even greater extent French Canadians crave the same within their own jurisdiction.

Canada is not, as has been often stressed, an entirely precise mosaic of nations; in fact, it is, like the U.S.A., gradually becoming a melting pot of nationalities, the difference between the two countries being that whereas the United States and the individual provinces of Canada allow their various national groups to exist and develop their national cultures, only Canada has recently begun meagrely to assist them materially in their specific endeavours. Now that the Bilingual and Bicultural Commission has performed its task and established in Canada the concept of a nation composed of two founding races, it could not but recognize the existence of a third multicultural fragmented segment which has the democratic right to preserve its freedom of independent action in matters linguistic and cultural, provided it preserves the spirit of Canadianism and does not go against the grain of the nation's constituted authority. A special ministry has even been created to cater to the necessities of that many-textured nationalistic miscellany to support their cultural inheritances. However, the support granted them remains, and perhaps will remain, a mere pittance, a small gesture of kindness on the part of the government, perhaps simply to humour them for the time being. The colourful and picturesque cultural activities of these ethnic entities are admired by Anglo-Saxons, but it is unlikely that they will ever become incorporated in the general Canadian culture. In a word, Canada is, in fact, a dual country and will increasingly be so until these non-English and non-French communities eventually become totally assimilated into either of these races' ways of life. Unless the Canadian government allows more immigration from Europe and other parts of the world, and unless the so-called Iron Curtain is raised to permit a greater emigration, the Anglo-Saxon and the English-speaking population in Canada in general will, in the next few decades, gain in numbers and, through intermarriages, engulf the ethnic groups into the vast sea of Anglicism in which the national racial elements, now conscious of their descent, will forget their backgrounds and will in no way differ from the English mode of civic life. To what extent the French in Quebec will succeed in that respect, is a difficult question to answer, because the newcomers tend much more greatly towards the English-speaking multitude even in that linguistically separate Province.

If a certain degree of favour on the part of the Anglo-Saxon and French predominant elements towards the Slavs and other ethnic varieties is to be detected, the former two (even if, for the sake of emphasis, we run the risk of being repetitive in this case), particularly the French, pay but scant attention to the latter, for they foresee that their concern with them will not last too long. To the French, all the races inhabiting Canada, except the English-speaking one, are only a hindrance which will disappear once all ethnicity in Canada vanishes. This disappearance, in the form of assimilation, is now taking place by leaps and bounds.

To revert to our previous discussion, a trickle of Slavic immigrants in the eighties of the nineteenth century followed much greater numbers of Icelanders, both of whom settled mainly in the West. Other national European clusters did the same. But it must be remembered that a certain number of them all arrived in Canada much earlier, in the first half of the century, and preferred to make their homes in the industrialized urban centres of eastern regions, mostly in Toronto and southern Ontario. There, being almost completely surrounded by the English-speaking people, they became the more readily integrated with them. Immigrants settling in the West, of course, did not find themselves in such surroundings and, as a result, had a greater opportunity to preserve their manners and customs than did their eastern compatriots. The loneliness of the farmers, who lived few and far between on the western plains, evoked in them the feeling of nostalgia which the more literate of them poured out into tearful folklorist lyrics, expressing in them an ardent desire to return to their native regions in the Old Country; or if they lived relatively closer together, to recreate an atmosphere of their abandoned homelands where, despite their poverty, they still enjoyed the pleasure of intimacy with those who shared their speech and culture. The western settlers in particular sought to preserve that kind of cultural climate wherever they situated themselves. It can be said that all the immigrants in Canada, with but very few exceptions, experienced that depressed feeling, but if one were to judge by the primitive poetry of most of them, the Ukrainian settlers surpassed all the others in that respect. And what else could be expected of

37

them? One of them related to this writer how he and his family were brought by an agent in an ox-driven wagon to their homestead in the wilderness that was then Saskatchewan and were virtually "dumped" there to fend for themselves as best they could. What could they do, the man said, but fall to their knees and in a fervent prayer to God ask Him to help sustain themselves on this uninhabited and uncultivated land. Believing that Providence ministers to those who minister to themselves, this family immediately began to build a shelter and, having constructed it, started the arduous work of clearing the harsh land for cultivation.

All their misfortunes, particularly of those Ukrainians who arrived here before and shortly after the First World War, are set forth in brief quatrains most of them without much care being given to their rhyme and rhythm, and—often—to reason. They were adapted to the "kolomiyka" tunes that served them as an accompaniment to their whirling dances in the Old Country. In spite of their generally melancholy and nostalgic content, these tunes were somewhat merry and, strangely enough, many were in a major key. The Ukrainians who immigrated to Canada between the two Wars were more broadly and better educated than their predecessors and, if some felt literary enough, they wrote their verses in a more intellectual and objective manner. A few of the authors of that period produced poetry which could now be termed as fairly subjective and but a step or two from genuine lyricism. The same could be said of the settlers of other national origins who, like the Ukrainians, experienced unhappy conditions in their incipient nation.

Russian immigrants were composed mostly of "Doukhobors" (the spirit-wrestlers) who, on account of their *quasi*-Tolstoyan religious tenets, suffered persecution in tsarist Russia and were practically forced to seek peace and freedom in Canada. There are about thirty thousand of them here. Some of them settled approximately eighty years ago as farmers in central Saskatchewan, and others, especially those calling themselves "Sons of Freedom" (really Old Believers) in British Columbia, principally in its Kootenay Valley region. If one compares them with over one million of other Slavs in Canada, the "Doukhobors" are a small but vocal minority, having contributed very little to the cultural development of Canada. If any writing has been done by them, it has been in the field of polemics, as one of their sects fiercely attacked another and vice-versa. For Canada this manner of conduct meant only trouble.

It must, however be borne in mind that there are well over one

38

hundred thousand non-sectarian Russians in Canada, and their positive activities are well described by H. Okulevich in his *Russians in Canada* (published in Toronto in 1952). In it, among quite a number of Russian professionals, such as artists, lawyers, engineers, medical doctors, and all sorts of scientists, only one Canadian Russian poet is mentioned, N. N. Popoff. In his excerpt from "To the Young Man" he exhorts young people not to waste their time in idle amusements, but to work seriously for the good of the scattered communities of his race. Furthermore, this brief extract reveals Popoff as a fine master of rhyme and rhythm. If he produced any more poetry of this type, it may now lie scattered in the Russian newspaper *Kanadskiy Gudok*. It should eventually be collected into a volume which would certainly prove the crowning glory of the Russian, including "Doukhobor," population in Canada.

Among other Russian "Doukhobor" authors writing in British Columbia are I. Sysoev, A. Konkin, V. Makhonin and several others whose rather ragged poetry and prose are published in a mimeographed religious weekly *Iskra*.

A Russian Canadian poet who is to be estimated of much greater stature than any of those just mentioned is Leonid Strakhovsky (1898-1963) whose collection *Dolg Zhizni* (The Debt to Life), published in Toronto in 1953, is written in a plaintive mood as he reminisces about his youthful years in Russia. He is not at all interested in Canadian life. His entire poetic and prose work seems to glorify the Russian tsarist past whose downfall he bemoans bitterly. His master in poetry is N. Gumilev whose "Acmeism" he slavishly imitates. Much of his writings Strakhovsky published in a biennial journal *Sovremennik* (The Contemporary), in which were also printed the musical verses of Canada's greatest Russian poetess, Ella Bobrova.

Among the various ethnic communities in Canada, it would not be an exaggeration to state that the Ukrainians were, and still are, the most active in matters literary. No sooner did they establish themselves in this country than those who were most poetically inclined among them began to pour out their sorrows in the primitive "kolomiyka" style, a trochaic ballad measure mentioned above. Much of this kind of poetry was published in several newspapers which started to appear at the turn of this century. According to Dr. Kirkconnell, about ten thousand of these lyrical items now moulder on the yellowed pages in newspaper offices, especially in Winnipeg.

The first collection of such verses, entitled *The Immigrants'*

39

Songs, in which their pioneering effort revealed itself, was published in Winnipeg in 1911. Its author and compiler was Theodore Fedik (1873-1949) who, in addition to his own lyrics, added several other minor ones by those who, like him, lessened their griefs by writing about their hardships in cultivating the stubbornly unyielding land, or toiling on the railroad, in mines, and in lumber camps. This paperback collection was truly a human document, and it is no wonder that by 1927 it had gone through four editions, selling well over fifty thousand copies. It is no longer as popular as it was then, but preserves its antiquarian value nonetheless and is inestimable to one who wishes to discover how these despised, weary, hungry immigrants felt as they sought their consolation in composing these often lugubrious folksongs by which the first pioneers, oddly enough, were uplifted and strengthened in their hope of better days to come. Better times did gradually come as the second, third, and now fourth generations of Ukrainians set about to assert themselves in practically all aspects of Canadian life.

Vassil Kudrik, in his *Vesna* (The Spring), also published in 1911, continued to poetize in the same manner but, being a finer craftsman, on a somewhat higher level. To the pathetic verses characterizing the pioneering spirit he added historical, social, political, and religious themes. Later, after a goodly part of Ukrainians separated from the Greek Catholic Church in Canada and established their native Orthodoxy, Kudrik became an inveterate polemicist against the former rite and ended his life as a staunch antagonist of the Ukrainian Uniate Church.

Sentimental poetry continued to be written, but not to that degree of intensity as initially. One comes across the names of such writers as J. Yasenchuk, the author of *Canadian Kobzar*, published in Edmonton in 1918; V. K. Holovatsky, D. Rarahovsky, and P. Crath, all co-authors in *Workers' Songs* (Winnipeg, 1911); and a playwright, S. Kowbel, who also wrote fine lyrics. The greatest were Ivan Danylchuk and Honoré Ewach, both up to the thirties the best Ukrainian Canadian poets of the Romantic school. But surpassing even these two was Ivan Kmeta-Efimovich, who can be truly regarded as a first-rank poet of the impressionistic type which at times bordered on sheer abstract phraseology.

There were several Ukrainian prose writers of note, but none to compare with Ilya Kiryak (1888-1955) who created one of the greatest epics to be written in Canada, *Syny zemli* (Sons of the Soil), a work of three volumes comprising some eleven hundred pages and published in Winnipeg between 1934 and 1945. In the sixties it was translated into English by M. Luchkovich (the first Ukrainian member of the House of Commons) and published in a somewhat fragmentary abbreviated version in Toronto towards the end of the past decade. In his work Kiryak described in great detail the settlement of the first Ukrainian pioneers in Alberta, their gradual integration into the Canadian manner of life, and, above all, their incipient and expanding Canadianism which, however, did not preclude the retention of their own cultural heritage. Three generations of Canadian Ukrainians pass before one's imagination, each outdoing the previous one in material and spiritual achievements. The episodes presented in this opus are of great interest, especially those that divulge the cordial relations between the newcomers and the English-speaking communities, the latter being collectively represented by the teacher, a Mr. Goodwin, a student from an eastern Canadian university. A passage of profound distinction is the marriage of an Anglo-Saxon into a Ukrainian family, which event, some forty years ago, and occasionally even much later, was considered by the Ukrainians as a tragedy. Kiryak resolved the problem by having the marriage ceremony performed according to the Ukrainian Byzantine rite. The novel ends just as World War II begins, at the time when the pioneers' sons are getting ready to depart for the European front in order to defend the freedom they and their parents enjoy in Canada. Certain Ukrainian critical enthusiasts compare this epic to Tolstoy's *War and Peace*. Such a comparison, however, is a faltering one. Regardless of how admirably Kiryak presented four decades of Ukrainian life in this country, he cannot be called a second Tolstoy. Nevertheless, he is the most eminent Ukrainian-Canadian novelist and his work may well be placed beside similar works by the first-rate Anglo-Saxon or French men of letters, particularly on a par with Louis Hémon's *Maria Chapdelaine*.

Many names crowd one's memory as one tries to select at least a few who can be located within the circle of universal poets. A limit must be placed on three of such a calibre. Reverend Stefan Semchuk (1899-   ) was perhaps the first to treat Canadian themes and rejoice in the beauty of Canadian nature, much more so than any other of his stamp. M. I. Mandryka (1886-   ) may also be considered as universal in that he deals philosophically and aesthetically with whatever subjects his mind can seize, be they natural, spiritual, or exotic. Sentimentally he is still attached to his native land, but he is fully aware that he is now a Canadian first and foremost. The same applies to Yar Slavutych (1918-   ) who as a styl-

41

ist is second to none among his fellow poets. An extensive compilation of his poems and lyrics is contained in a volume he named *Trofeyi* (The Trophies) which is certainly his greatest achievement on the scale of sheer catholicity. In his lengthy poem *Zavoyovnyky preriy* (The Conquerors of the Prairies) he, more than any other writer, except perhaps Kiryak, lavishly depicts the pioneering spirit of the Canadian West. According to Dr. Mandryka, "Slavutych is a poet by the grace of God. His creative poetical power consists of a happy synthesis of heart, spirit, and mind, enlightened by learning. . . . " All these three men of letters practise a variety of styles— Classical, Romantic, Impressionistic, Expressionistic; and oftentimes one finds in them even tinges of abstract notions. Their serious writings began between the two World Wars and still continue to thrive at the present time.

Among a certain number of Canadian-born writers of Ukrainian extraction the following deserve honourable mention. Myra Lazechko-Haas began to write poetry in Winnipeg when she was only nine. Her first poem was printed by the *Winnipeg Free Press* and her other lyrics appeared in the *Calgary Herald* and in the *Globe and Mail*. In 1952 the former Ryerson Press published her *Chapbook of Poetry* which received but scanty attention, mainly because her abstract manner of thinking makes her works incomprehensible to most lovers of poetry. At present she is not as prolific as she was in past years.

Another author is Vasyl Paluk who, in 1943, published his *Ukrainian Cossacks* in Winnipeg. It is a brief volume of only 134 pages in which are collected several articles on Ukrainian topics and three short stories likewise dealing with the hardships undergone by his people during the pioneering period. Although he has written several dramatic pieces for television (only two with regard to Ukrainians), he is to be pronounced as a *homo unius libri* in which he reveals himself as a fairly good psychoanalyst.

Vera Lysenko's *The Men in Sheepskin Coats* and *Yellow Boots*, published in 1942 and 1954 respectively by the former Ryerson Press, are her most important volumes. In the first, Miss Lysenko, according to her critics, describes the first Ukrainian settlements and their organization into various societies in a manner detrimental to their social respect. There was quite an uproar among Canadian Ukrainians when this book appeared. In the second, she presents a Ukrainian girl who becomes a fine singer thanks to non-Ukrainian assistance, but who, despite the lack of interest of her own people in her career, still contributes to their folk art which, together with the yellow (ornamented) boots worn on festive occasions, is their precious national heritage. The upshot of this novel's plot seems to be that Canadians, regardless of their national extraction, would do well to become heterogeneous ethnically, if not wholly assimilated.

By this time it becomes fairly evident that those authors who have written about their national groups have dealt mostly with the process of their immigration and with the historical aspects of their life in Canada. Whatever literary endeavour they have shown has been, to a large extent, considered as secondary to their material accomplishments. This was precisely the case in regard to Polish immigrants. If it had not been for Dr. Kirkconnell, we would know precious little of their limited literary output in this country. To be sure, there have appeared several books on how the Polish cultural organizations came to be, but this can hardly be placed in the belletristic category. It is apparent that the Poles in Canada, as in some measure other ethnic communities, nurtured themselves spiritually mostly on their rich national literature already produced in Europe, and only passably betook themselves to create their own original poetry and fiction in the land of their adoption. Only a few Canadian Polish literary works are known to us.

In his "Slavic Literatures in Canada," an essay published in *Slavs in Canada,* Vol. I in Edmonton, 1966, Professor Yar Slavutych mentions several titles that appeared in the Polish language here; but the authors of those books, with one or two exceptions, are but little noted for producing genuine masterpieces. Arkady Fiedler (1894-   ), who lived in Canada for a brief while, published, in 1937, a chronicle of his passage through Canada, entitled *Kanada pachnacą zywicą* (Canada Smelling of Resin) which proved interesting enough to gain seven or eight editions. In 1964, Aleksander Grobnicki wrote and published in Toronto his *Wojenne blyski* (Flashes of War), dealing with the Polish activities in the second Armageddon. Among the poets, Slavutych mentions such names as Marian Lisowski who wrote *Wrocimy* (We Shall Return) which was published in Windsor, Ontario in 1942, and Aleksander Janta whose *Widzenie Wiary* (A Vision of Faith) appeared in Montreal in 1946. S. Michalski belongs to the abstractionist and ultra-modernistic poets, and wrote mostly satirical verses, as is revealed in his *Garbuz i garby* (Hunchback and Humps) which was published in Montreal in 1962 and figures prominently among his prolific verses. Perhaps the greatest Polish poetess in Canada is Danata Bienkowska whose philosophic muse,

43

as Slavutych judges it, "sinks down deeply into the reader's mind." Another poetess of eminent worth is Romualda Bromke whose chief work, *Rymy moje* (My Rhymes), was written in an impressionistic mood. Franciszek Kmietorowicz wrote what was said to be the finest Polish novel in Canada, *Gwiazdy nad Toronto* (The Stars over Toronto). Unfortunately, it seems to have been lost, as it could not be found in any of the libraries in Western Canada. Perhaps it still exists in some obscure Polish library in another part of the country. He was also the author of *Kanadyjski oberek* (A Canadian Oberek). Oberek is a typically Polish whirling dance. This book is a collection of sketches and short stories in folklorist style. Much credit must go to the above mentioned Polish authors for their notable effort in seeking to construct their own Canadian literature. In all evidence, they are quite capable of achieving this aim. In conclusion to this section, one must not forget that Watson Kirkconnell wrote several books on Poland and translated quite an amount of Polish poetic material, thus bringing the Canadians of Polish descent to a greater understanding of those who are interested in the development of the Polish spirit within the framework of Canadianism.

While investigating foreign publications in Canada, Dr. Kirkconnell discovered that Rudolf Nekola was the first poet in Canada to publish a collection of his Czech poetry. This event occurred in Montreal in 1943, and the small volume was entitled *Noc v hore Kralovské* (A Night on Mount Royal). Despite his poems being nostalgic in nature, they nevertheless bear the stamp of a Canadian spirit in that in them he describes the places he visited in the new land of his choice. Another poet of note is Professor J. Skvor who wrote his lyrics after World War II under the pseudonym of Pavel Javor. He published two selections of verse in Toronto—*Daleky hlas* (The Distant Voice) in 1953, and *Horke verse* (Bitter Verses) in 1958. Two years later, there appeared in New York his *Kour z Ithaky* (The Smoke from Ithaca), a selection from his lyrical output in the fifties, in which the age he lived in evoked in him a gloomy imagination with regard to humanity's bleak future. This anthology, whose first poem was translated by Dr. Kirkconnell, had a great impact not only upon the Canadian Czechs but likewise on Slavic literature in general.

Slovak literature in Canada is conspicuously more prolific than the Czech. Almost all of its poets wrote after World War II, and their poetry as a whole is distinguished by its polished manner. Among them are O. M. Debnarkin whose first collection in this country, *Zjavnym hlasom* (With Distinct Voice), was printed in

1952. It is meditative in tone and philosophic in content. Cyril Ondruc's work reveals an intense love for his native country. J. Dragos-Alsbetinkan, a priest, based his poetry on heroic and historical themes of Slovakia. One of his collections, *Slavne hviezdy jasne* (Glorious Bright Stars), which appeared in 1963, contains perhaps his greatest poem, a religious panegyric to Saints Cyril and Methodius, two Greeks who in the eighth century came from Thessalonica to the region in central Europe then called Pannonia (which embraces the present Slovakia and part of Hungary) and converted the races inhabiting it to Christianity. In addition, they invented for the Slavs an alphabet which, with but minor changes, is still used today by most of the Slavic nations. Although L. Benesovsky published his novels in Europe, their influence on Canadian Slovaks was great. He also wrote numerous lyrics and poems which are scattered in Slovak newspapers and journals and await their publication in book form. J. Z. Tien is both a poet and a dramatist. His versified drama, *Ohne* (The Flames), was published in Winnipeg in 1955. It teems with intense patriotism as he recounts the liberation movement in his native land, and continues to exert a profound influence on his compatriots wherever they live. The same may be said of J. Doransky who, in addition to dramas, writes fine lyric poetry. Although he is not a literary figure in the full sense of the term, one is compelled in this instance to mention Dr. Joseph Kirschbaum, a first-rate historian and scholar in other cultural fields. More than anyone else, it is he who has really introduced the Slovaks to other Canadians by means of his erudite works.

It is interesting to note that the Croatian authors, of whom only two are generally known to Canadian Slavists, have contributed more to French Canadian than to English Canadian literature. Nadia Stipkovic is the author of the collection of poems entitled *Lignes*. Alain Horic has been writing in French during the past twenty years. His first collection of poetry, published in Montreal in 1957, bears the heading *L'Aube assassiné*. The second fascicle of verse which appeared in 1962, likewise in Montreal, he called *Blessure au flanc du ciel*. Both these books were sponsored by the Canada Council. Since six of his poems were included in the *Anthologie de littérature du Québec,* and inasmuch as all his poems are considered favourably by French Canadian critics, it is to be assumed that he has really had a certain influence on French Canadian literature. Horic is a Bosnian and a Moslem, and his poetry is somewhat melancholy in tone.

Deluged by the flood of literature realized by the ethnic popula-

45

tions in Canada, its "third segment," one might ask what influence has it bestowed on Anglo- and French-Canadian fine letters? At this point one must first consider how much of it has been translated into English or French. Concerning French Canadians, it may be stated offhand that, with but very few exceptions just mentioned, its instrumentality has been almost nil. They seem to be uninterested in any ethnic literature but their own, and their literati have not yet taken enough pains to discover what lies beyond the ken of their own accomplishments in literary and cultural fields. What is written in English, however, stirs them to a lesser or greater degree.

The English-speaking population, on the other hand, was fortunate in having inquisitive men and, occasionally, women of letters who did their best to discover at least a small amount in foreign literatures in Canada to their compatriots. Among them was A. J. Hunter who, having learned the Ukrainian language tolerably well, translated short selections from Taras Shevchenko's poetry which was published in Manitoba as early as 1922 under the title of *The Kobzar of Ukraine*. There followed Percival Cundy whose *Voice of Ukrainia* comprised a selection of Ivan Franko's lyrics as well as a comprehensive introduction to that poet's works. Franko's verse he later expanded in *Ivan Franko, Poems* (1949). Subsequently (1950), Cundy issued *Spirit of Flame*, containing a very small fraction of Lesya Ukrainka's poetry. Three of this poetess' dramas and a few of her lyrical pieces were transmuted into English by Vera Rich (who resides in England), and published in 1968 under the title of *Lesya Ukrainka, Selected Works* by the University of Toronto Press. This translation is preceded by Dr. Constantine Bida's extensive introduction, which deals with this author's life and works. In his original labours Dr. G. W. Simpson concerned himself mainly with Ukrainian cultural, historical, and geographical matters. Florence Randal Livesay, to the best of her intent, and with the assistance of P. Crath, rendered into English, in 1940, H. Kvitka-Osnovianenko's *Marusia*, the first novel to be written in the Ukraine. This was followed by her *Songs of Ukraina*, a short anthology of that country's folklorist poetry.

But the greatest among the translators was Dr. Watson Kirkconnell, who did not limit himself simply to Ukrainian writers, but encompassed in his brilliant renditions literary selections from many other national groups whose languages, we repeat, he mastered expressly for that purpose. His surveys of *Publications in*

Other Languages, which he published in the *University of Toronto Quarterly* annually from 1937 to 1966, form a vast compendium of what had been written in various idioms in Canada during these three decades. As a whole, this continuous work presents to the English-speaking community inestimable and indispensable bibliographical material which those who are interested in other literatures may consult at will. His *Canadian Overtones* similarly reveal his scholarly curiosity in the multicultural phases of Canadian literary activity.

Considering his translations from other, Canadian or European, literatures, one must not overlook his English versions of certain European poets. Among them stands out the name of the greatest Polish poet, Adam Mickiewicz, whose famous epic *Pan Tadeusz*, completed and published in 1834, is considered by many to be the greatest in this genre in the Slavic world. Dr. Kirkconnell had translated it by 1962 and saw it published that year by the University of Toronto Press under the auspices of the Millenium of Christian Poland Celebration Committee. This work of his received a favourable review in the London *Times Literary Supplement*, October 12, 1962. His other translations are included in such collections as *A Polish Miscellany, A Magyar Miscellany, European Elegies, North American Book of Icelandic Verse, The Magyar Muse: an Anthology of Hungarian Poetry 1400-1932, A Golden Treasury of Polish Lyrics, A Little Treasury of Hungarian Verse*, János Arany's *The Death of King Buda: a Hungarian Epic Poem* (with Lulu Payerle), *Prince Ihor's Raid against the Polovtsi: a Slavic Epic* (with P. Crath). This list is by no means exhaustive, and finding Kirkconnell so versatile and profuse, facetiously speaking, one is tempted to say not *et cetera*, but *ad infinitum*. His greatest contribution to the Ukrainians is his translation (in collaboration with C. H. Andrusyshen) of selections from over one hundred Ukrainian poets. This volume, *Ukrainian Poets 1189-1962*, published in 1963 by the University of Toronto Press, which is so active in matters Slavic, comprises 500 pages and presents a vast panorama of Ukrainian historical, social, philosophical, and religious thought, a work such as had never before been attempted. His other voluminous undertaking was *The Complete Poetical Works of Taras Shevchenko: the Kobzar* (likewise with the same collaborator and publisher, and 560 pages in length). The latter volume commemorates the one hundred and fiftieth anniversary of the poet's birth. How these two important works came into being is very interestingly described in Kirkconnell's *A Slice of*

Canada. In that reference, I wish only to repeat the chief translator's justly stated boast that whereas it took Alexander Pope, with several assistants, twelve years to complete an English verse translation of Homer, totalling less than one thousand pages, Andrusyshen and he completed their two bulky volumes, considerably longer than the *Iliad* and the *Odyssey* combined, within only fifteen months.

Such, then, is Watson Kirkconnell's immense accomplishment for the benefit of Canadian ethnic masses in general. For him it was not only a fascinating job, for in dealing with the literatures of the peoples of various origins in Canada, he learned much that was historically and culturally new to him; it was also an altruistic task, for, as he performed it, he knew that he was laying the foundations for the edification of the future generations of those national entities with whom he was concerned and who in the well recognized process of time would become merged into purely Anglo-Saxon Canadianism. The problem to be resolved was how the present and future generations, having forgotten the speech of their forefathers, might yet retain the national spirit of their respective races. The expectation was that, by reading in English what their predecessors have created in Canada in their original languages, one might hope that the assimilation of the present ethnic elements would not be total. It may be believed that Watson Kirkconnell's aim in doing what he did was to begin a trend whereby all ethnic cultures, even if they became thoroughly Canadianized, would at least still be aware of their ancestral heritage in the decades and, one hopes, centuries to come.

What impact these ethnic literatures, whether in the original or in translation, have, or will have, on Anglo- or French-Canadian literature is a moot question. Thus far their influence has not been significant, for English-speaking Canadians, with but few exceptions, are not willing to learn Slavic languages; and, on the other hand, the members of those ethnic groups who have not yet become assimilated, thus far do not appear to express their ideas and ideals in English strongly enough to be heard and heeded. Dr. Kirkconnell and those like him do their utmost in this multicultural task; but what can a mere handful do to persuade their fellow-countrymen to immerse themselves in the literatures of the "foreign" elements whom the Anglo-Saxons and French Canadians, in spite of the protestations to the contrary, look upon, at best, as second-rate citizens? According to the leaders of ethnic communities, it is just so.

In the past eighty years, since the tides of immigration from Europe and other parts of the world began to swell the population of Canada, it has not yet, even after this goodly lapse of time, become evident that the two founding races have been appreciably inspired by the newcomers' spiritual ideals expressed in their various literatures and cultures. Rather than being influenced by them, they have only become more aware of their existence. In natural and technological sciences, however, matters are quite different. In ever greater numbers those of central and eastern European stock continue to excel in them and, naturally enough, their researches and discoveries are encouraged and willingly accepted by all scientists. In the realm of letters, however, the immigrant literatures are rated to be of an inferior category. This may have been true to some degree in the past when, it cannot be denied, they did vegetate on a humble level. But the time has now come when new authors, descendants of the early settlers in Canada, have appeared. They are steeped in new ideas and understand modern literary trends. Their ever-improving English is becoming a vehicle whereby they are ready to translate their aims and aspirations to their fellow-Canadians of other races, and to share their novel perceptions with them. However, in many cases, it will come to pass only when ethnic literatures have been transmitted to Anglo-Saxons and French Canadians in the languages which the latter two will understand. Then all Canadians, no matter how diverse in origin, will be in a position to exchange and enjoy the ideals inherent in all literatures, be they of greater or lesser magnitudes.

Les Humanités dans l'enseignement supérieur au Canada

par Maurice Lebel, D. Litt. F.R.S.C.

Les humanités, les *studia humanitatis, humaniores disciplinae*, comme on les appelait jadis, occupent depuis longtemps une place importante dans l'enseignement secondaire, collégial, et supérieur au Canada. De Terre-Neuve à Victoria, *a mari usque ad mare*, les humanités gréco-latines, païennes, et chrétiennes, anciennes et médiévales, d'Homère à Dante et Chaucer, sont enseignées au pays, où elles font aussi l'objet de recherches et de publications scientifiques. Les humanités modernes, qui vont de la Renaissance à nos jours, sont également étudiées et inspirent d'innombrables mouvements et projets, publications et sociétés savantes; elles sont même devenues aujourd'hui si riches et si variées qu'elles sont en train de former une entité distincte, indépendante des humanités anciennes et médiévales, puis des humanités modernes issues de la Renaissance des XVe et XVIe siècles.

Nous assistons, en effet, surtout depuis un quart de siècle, à la lente et sûre création de nouvelles humanités modernes, fondées principalement sur la production protéiforme, sur les découvertes et les inventions, les sciences et les techniques du XXe siècle. C'est que l'homme contemporain, ployant sous le poids de l'héritage du passé et désespérant de jamais pouvoir le connaitre, encore moins de l'approfondir, tend de plus en plus à se créer des humanités à son image et à sa resemblance, qui est celle d'un être éphémère, passager, tel un acteur sur la scène, et ainsi à limiter ses horizons à son milieu et à son temps. Comme pris de vertige et emporté dans un tourbillon par le développement spectaculaire de l'électronique et des *mass media* il est fortement tenté de prendre l'immédiat, l'instantané, le mouvement incessant de la vie pour l'essentiel et le permanent; il est porté à tenir l'observation et la critique de la société pour l'histoire et à couler son existence au gré des images, des sons, et des bruits qui sont devenus pour lui comme une seconde forme de pain quotidien; aveuglé qu'il est par le progrès matériel et la publicité tapageuse, il a peine à se rendre compte que mode et moderne sont presque synonymes. En effet, le mot moderne—d'après l'adjectif latin *modernus, a, um,* employé pour la première fois au VIe siècle de notre ère, au temps de l'empereur Justinien, par deux auteurs de basse latinité, Priscien de Césarée, grammairien de profession, et Cassiodore, historien, homme d'État, et moine—vient de deux mots latins, *modo* et *modus,* qui signifient respectivement il y a un instant, naguère, tout à l'heure, et manière, façon, forme, mode.

Parallèlement à cette forte tendance de l'homme contemporain à rompre en visière au passé et à étudier presque exclusivement son milieu et son temps, on constate, avec un plaisir mêlé de joie et d'émerveillement, un vif retour à l'étude de la Renaissance, de ses humanistes et de leurs oeuvres, et cela un peu partout, comme on en peut juger par la prolifération des colloques et des congrès sur la Renaissance, par la création et l'activité de centres d'études de la Renaissance avec bibliothèques spécialisées, bulletins, revues, et publications savantes. De même que les humanistes de la Renaissance étaient soucieux de renouer, par-dessus la scolastique et le Moyen Age, la culture moderne à la culture antique, de même bon nombre d'humanistes aujourd'hui travaillent à relier le monde du XXe siècle à celui de la Renaissance. D'autant plus que notre époque possède de nombreuses affinités avec celle de la Renaissance; beaucoup de problèmes du jour passionnaient déjà les esprits aux XVe et XVIe siècles. A vrai dire, nous assistons aujourd'hui à la naissance d'une seconde Renaissance.

Tels sont les principaux pôles d'attraction et les mouvements opposés qui attirent et partagent l'enseignement des humanités à l'heure actuelle. Le Canada, fidèle à ses origines—il est une création des XVIe et XVIIe siècles—continue de se pencher sur son passé. Il étudie aussi le présent et est tendu vers l'avenir. La Querelle des Anciens et des Modernes, loin d'être morte, y a pris une nouvelle tournure. Notre enseignement des humanités en porte la marque. Watson Kirkconnell, conscient de l'esprit nouveau qui soufflait déjà en 1943, prit alors l'initiative de réunir quelques collègues d'université et de créer avec eux le Conseil canadien de recherche en humanités, dont il fut le premier président. Un an plus tard, à l'automne de 1944, avec le concours inestimable de John E. Robbins et grâce à une généreuse subvention de la Fondation Rockefeller, de New York, il inaugurait une vaste enquête sur l'état présent des humanités au Canada. Des équipes de professeurs se partagèrent la tâche en 1945, visitant les différentes régions du pays, de l'est à l'ouest. Le rapport des enquêteurs, *The Humanities in Canada*,[1] parut à Ottawa en 1947 sous la signature de Watson Kirkconnel et de A.S.P. Woodhouse; le président actuel de l'Université de Windsor, John Francis Leddy, y contribua aussi un article intitulé: "The Place of the Humanities in Secondary Education."

The Humanities in Canada est beaucoup plus qu'une vue d'ensemble et une synthèse magistrale, truffée de bibliographies, de renseignements historiques, et de statistiques. Ce volume, non content d'être une enquête exacte et précise, la première du genre au pays à servir de modèle à d'autres par la suite et à être regardée d'un oeil d'envie par les spécialistes, constitue aussi une étape, telle une pierre blanche, dans l'histoire de l'enseignement et de l'érudition humanistes. Loin de se borner à décrire une situation de fait, il propose hardiment une vision des choses à venir, *a shape of things to come*; il révèle le pouvoir de l'imagination créatrice, marquée au coin de l'expérience et de la sagesse, en montrant la voie et en traçant les grandes lignes d'un programme d'action. Lisez, par exemple, la liste des recommandations (pp. 203-9), dont il demande l'application dans le plus bref délai possible. En voici quelques-unes, qui ont déjà fait époque: la création d'une bibliothèque nationale; la création d'un Conseil des arts, des humanités, et des sciences sociales; la formation d'associations de professeurs dans les disciplines suivantes: histoire, philosophie, lettres classiques, langues modernes, langues orientales, langues slaves, littérature comparée; l'enrichissement des bibliothèques; une enquête sur les archives dans les collèges et les universités; l'avancement des études chinoises, slaves, régionales, musicales; des bourses de recherches post-doctorales; des bourses de recherches en vue de la maîtrise et du doctorat; l'année sabbatique; la fondation de revues spécialisées; l'art dramatique; l'échange et la visite de professeurs; l'aide à la publication, l'encouragement à la création littéraire; un répertoire des thèses de maîtrise et de doctorat, puis la mise à jour annuelle de pareille liste; les relations du Conseil canadien de recherche en humanités avec l'American Council of Learned Societies, l'Union Académique internationale, et l'UNESCO. En bref, le rapport de 1947 est un magnifique exemple de prospective juste et mesurée; l'histoire lui a donné raison, la plupart de ses recommandations ayant été mises en marche depuis lors.

La majeure partie de la Préface, remarquable de limpidité et de plénitude, décrit la fonction des humanités et l'apport de l'enseignement des humanités à la vie nationale; elle mériterait encore, à elle seule, une réimpression et une large diffusion. Je m'en voudrais de ne point en citer ici quelques passages:

> We are in the midst of a movement that is reacting against excessive preoccupation with techniques divorced from humanizing influences and is demanding that education, especially higher education, shall liberalize or humanize the modern student, so as to educate the whole man and make him completely human, a representative of the universally human spirit. How is this universally human spirit to be imparted? In the past, it was with the great classics of antiquity that the student sought to merge his spirit. Association with the poets, orators, and historians of the past detached him from the mere present, humanized his imagination, and elevated his sentiments. Can this kind of effect be produced for us, not only by the classics of Greece and Rome but by the modern equivalents as well? Just what is the essential function of the humanities?
>
> The function of the humanities is to humanize by stimulating the imagination to develop in breadth and depth until the individual becomes enlarged into the full measure of humanity. In literature, by projecting ourselves imaginatively into the environment, the problems, and the characters created for us by the great masters, we enter vicariously into the whole range of human experience—extending, refining, and ennobling our feelings as we identify ourselves with this or that character, living with his life and growing with his growth.... History, with its historical point of view, added to such imaginative self-projection into literature, art and music, gives us perspective and a certain power of comparison and judgment of values; while philosophy not only enlarges our imagination but strengthens our powers of reflective and critical judgment in all fields of human experience. ... The humanities, more than any other studies, tend to

stimulate our sensitivity to the human values in art, morality and religion.

History and philosophy are disciplines that help to integrate other liberal disciplines in a larger pattern of chronological development and systematized comprehension. Historical perspective is important, since life in the present takes on a profounder meaning in the larger context of time, and since the humanistic disciplines are shallow and provincial when divorced from the artistic, moral, and religious heritage of the past. Philosophy, moreover, by its analysis of intellectual processes and its enquiries into the validity of knowledge, as well as by its critical clarification of definitions, concepts, and systems of thought in all fields of knowledge, appeals to the profound desire of a civilized man to co-ordinate his experiences of every sort into a well-rounded and coherent whole. . . .

All this points to an active function for the humanities in our time, not merely in entering effectively into the intellectual, esthetic, and moral legacy of the past but also in applying the resulting powers of the mind to the vast human needs and problems of the present.

En 1964, soit dix-sept ans après l'enquête de 1947, paraissait un deuxième volume également intitulé *The Humanities in Canada,* dû à la plume de F.E.L. Priestley.[2] Ce rapport, préparé pour le Conseil canadien de recherche en humanités, diffère sensiblement de celui de 1947. Il est centré exclusivement sur les humanités (programmes d'études, recherches, et publications) dans l'enseignement supérieur au Canada. Il traite de la situation générale, des problèmes communs aux universités, puis des recherches en cours et des publications, de 1947 à 1964. La bibliographie des recherches et des publications y occupe une place importante. Peu nombreux sont les tableaux statistiques, et il n'y est pas du tout question du développement historique des universités. D'ailleurs, celui-ci est énorme depuis 1947, et l'on peut être informé des plus récents progrès là-dessus en s'adressant, par exemple, à Statistique Canada, à la Fondation des Universités, à l'association des bibliothèques, ou encore à l'Association des collèges et des universités du Canada. Le rapport de 1964 révèle, par rapport à 1947, un accroissement prodigieux des disciplines, un élargissement de l'éventail des connaissances, notamment en art et en archéologie, dans les langues asiatiques et slaves, dans l'histoire des religions, les études sur l'Islam, la Renaissance, et l'Amérique latine. Par surcroît, la volumineuse bibliographie, suivie d'un Index, se présente sous les diverses rubriques suivantes: Classical and Mediaeval Studies, English Studies, Romance Languages, Other Modern Languages, Near Eastern Studies, Islamic Studies, Asian Studies, Philosophy, History, Fine Art and Varied Topics, Theology and History of Religion.

L'année 1966 vit paraître un troisième volume au titre identique, *The Humanities in Canada*, composé par R. M. Wiles, de regrettée mémoire, sur la demande expresse du Conseil canadien de recherche en humanités.[3] Ce livre comprend exclusivement, outre un Index, une bibliographie des publications savantes en guise de supplément à la bibliographie de 1964, dressée par F. E. L. Priestley. Ce complément, qui comprend plus de neuf cents nouveaux titres, est une contribution majeure à l'érudition et à l'humanisme au Canada.

Il reste encore, bien sûr, énormément de travail à accomplir. Il faudrait commencer par dresser la liste des recherches en cours et la bibliographie des livres parus au cours de la dernière décennie, de 1965 à nos jours. Le moment est arrivé aussi de faire le point dans l'enseignement des humanités, car celui-ci a évolué si rapidement depuis trente ans (1945-1975), à tous les niveaux: primaire, secondaire, et supérieur, que les enquêteurs de 1945 auraient peut-être aujourd'hui quelque gêne à se reconnaître dans la forêt des nouveaux bâtiments et programmes d'études. Les annuaires d'université ont pris beaucoup de poids. Les étudiants sont devenus si nombreux qu'ils doivent écrire les noms de trois universités sur un formulaire d'inscription avant de pouvoir être accepté par l'une d'elles; certains départements ont même dressé des barrières d'admission et établi un quota ou contingentement. Le nombre des professeurs a monté en flèche, à tel point que les départements d'histoire ou de langues modernes, du moins en bon nombre d'universités, comptent souvent à eux seuls jusqu'à 100, voire 150 et même 175 enseignants.[4] Les composantes des diplômes forment une vaste mosaïque par suite de la prolifération de la population scolaire et des nouvelles disciplines enseignées. La liste des bourses d'études et de recherches ressemble à une échelle mobile, digne de celle de Jacob. Est aussi longue la liste des auteurs de manuscrits qui demandent une aide à la publication et brûlent de voir leurs travaux paraître en librairie. Quelques esprits s'alarment même du foisonnement des sociétés savantes.[5]

Les revues savantes[6] ont aussi considérablement augmenté

depuis trente ans; quelques-unes d'entre elles se sont même taillé une haute réputation dans le monde scientifique.

L'enseignement des humanités a subi, lui aussi, de profondes modifications depuis trente ans. Il ne saurait être question pour moi de décrire à cette place l'état présent de la situation à cet égard; le sujet mériterait une vaste enquête, dont l'ampleur dépasserait de beaucoup celle de 1945. Tout au plus devrai-je me contenter d'un rapide survol, forcément incomplet, qui portera sur les études anciennes et médiévales, puis sur la Renaissance et les humanités modernes, enfin sur les études canadiennes.

Le grec et le latin sont de moins en moins enseignés à l'heure présente dans les écoles secondaires, les high schools, et les collèges. Sans être complètement disparus du curriculum de l'enseignement secondaire et collégial, ils n'y occupent plus une place de choix; la plupart des jeunes qui s'inscrivent aujourd'hui ignorent jusqu'aux caractères de l'alphabet grec, et beaucoup même savent peu de latin. En thèse générale, ils connaissent toutefois l'histoire ancienne d'Egypte et d'Israël, de Grèce et de Rome; ils croient, du moins pour l'avoir entendu dire en salle de classe, que ces divers pays sont à l'origine de la civilisation occidentale à laquelle ils appartiennent. S'ils ont peu ou point lu et traduit de textes anciens, si leur connaissance directe des langues et des littératures anciennes est mince, ils ne sont pas cependant sans avoir pratiqué les oeuvres de plusieurs auteurs grecs et latins en traduction. Pour avoir suivi des exposés de civilisation gréco-romaine, ils se sont intéressés quelque temps aux moeurs et aux coutumes, aux institutions privées et publiques, à la mythologie et aux pratiques religieuses des Anciens, voire à leur expression de l'art et à leurs grandes créations artistiques.[7] En bref, loin d'ignorer d'où ils viennent, ils ont quelque idée de la source de leur langue et de leur foi, de leur histoire et de leur littérature, de leur mentalité et de leur tournure d'esprit; pour eux, le Canada est une création de l'Europe et, à ce titre, se rattache à l'Occident.[8]

Ce qui frappe aussi, dans l'état présent des humanités grécolatines, c'est de voir s'élever chaque année le nombre des grands débutants qui s'attaquent à pied d'oeuvre à l'étude du grec et du latin à l'université. Sans doute conscients de leurs lacunes ou désireux de rattraper le temps employé autrement, en outre fortement motivés dans leurs études, ils s'adonnent aux langues anciennes avec une ardeur communicative et y font des progrès sensationnels en peu de temps.[9] Ces grands débutants sont plus qu'une précieuse addition aux étudiants réguliers de grec et de latin; ils sont aujourd'hui un stimulant de qualité et permettent aux professeurs de mesurer le développement intellectuel des uns par rapport aux autres. Ils s'apparentent aussi, pourrait-on dire, à ceux qui optent pour le grec biblique ou l'hébreu, le copte ou le syriaque, les langues sémitiques. Le nombre des étudiants et des chercheurs, habiles à maîtriser ces langues pourtant peu faciles, a augmenté considérablement au cours de ces dernières années. Le grec byzantin, le latin médiéval, le chinois médiéval sont loin d'être indifférents à beaucoup d'esprits, que ceux-ci soient des littéraires, des historiens, ou des philosophes. Il va sans dire que les cours d'introduction à la lecture et à l'étude des classiques en traduction continuent d'attirer des foules d'étudiants, notamment des écoles ou des facultés professionnelles.

L'archéologie classique, biblique, et méditerranéenne, la civilisation gréco-romaine, l'histoire ancienne, la patrologie grecque et latine attirent aussi beaucoup d'étudiants. Je pourrais nommer d'affilée, par exemple, une douzaine d'universités actuellement responsables de fouilles à Chypre, en Grèce, en Israël, en Italie, en France, au Liban, en Syrie, en Turquie, voire en Iran et en Afrique du Nord. D'autres universités organisent chaque été, les unes, des cours de vacances à Athènes ou à Rome, les autres, des stages d'études en Provence ou en Italie du Sud, celles-ci, des croisières en Méditerranée, celles-là, des visites guidées en Afrique du Nord. La mythologie, la Bible, l'art antique, le théâtre grec et latin, la littérature scientifique et l'histoire des sciences dans l'Antiquité, les philosophes pré-socratiques, Platon et Aristote, le néo-platonisme, la psychologie rationelle, l'art, l'histoire, la littérature et la philosophie du Moyen Age: voilà autant de sujets recherchés des étudiants. Le centre de traitement informatique de plusieurs universités, mobilisant plusieurs dizaines de chercheurs, a déjà commencé, par exemple, de mettre sur cartes perforées les soixante-dix traités d'Hippocrate ou de dresser la bibliographie la plus exhaustive des Pères de l'Eglise grecque et latine.[10] Bien connues sont les savantes publications de l'Institut Pontifical des Etudes Médiévales de l'Université de Toronto.[11] En bref, contrairement à ce que disent ou pensent des esprits chagrins, *laudatores temporis acti*, la situation des études anciennes et médiévales est loin d'être désespérée et perdue à jamais dans l'enseignement supérieur au Canada; plus de deux cents étudiants—ce sont *the happy few*—y sont inscrits cette année à la maîtrise ou au doctorat en études anciennes ou médiévales.

Pas davantage ne sont négligées les études de la Renaissance, à en juger par la création et l'essor des Centres d'études de la Renaissance, notamment en Ontario et au Québec. La traduction ou l'édition des textes des écrivains ou des humanistes de la Renaissance, tels que Budé[12] et Érasme,[13] Sir Thomas More et Roger Ascham,[14.] Sir Philip Sidney[15] et Sir Walter Raleigh,[16.] Ben Jonson, Spenser et Milton, Machiavel, Desportes, Ronsard, le théâtre et la critique littéraire de la Renaissance, la Renaissance anglaise et française, espagnole et italienne, l'humanisme de la Renaissance: tout cela fait l'objet d'enseignement, de recherches, et de publications. Paul Chavy, professeur à l'Université Dalhousie, Halifax, va bientôt publier la bibliographie des traductions françaises du XVIe siècle.[17]

Les humanités modernes et les études canadiennes occupent aujourd'hui une place de choix dans l'enseignement supérieur au Canada. L'étude des principales langues et littératures modernes d'Amérique, d'Asie, et d'Europe attire chaque année un nombre grandissant d'étudiants. En 1945, il y a trente ans, lors de la première enquête sur les humanités au Canada, celles-ci comprenaient principalement les disciplines suivantes: les langues et les littératures, la philologie, la philosophie, l'histoire, la religion, la musique, et le théâtre. L'essai de définition et de classification des humanités, tel que proposé par le Conseil canadien de recherche en humanités dans son premier rapport de 1947, est aujourd'hui dépassé et mériterait d'être mis à jour, eu égard au nouveau contexte. En plus des disciplines déjà mentionnées, voici celles qui sont dispensées aujourd'hui sous le nom d'humanités et font l'objet d'études spécialisées: l'histoire contemporaine, l'histoire des sciences, la philosophie des sciences, la bibliothéconomie, l'archivistique, l'étude des religions, la traduction et l'interprétariat, la littérature orale, le folklore, la linguistique, l'histoire de l'enseignement, le journalisme, la littérature comparée, le droit comparé, le droit canon, le droit international, l'histoire de l'art, les arts graphiques, plastiques, visuels, les communications de masse, le cinéma, la photographie, l'esthétique, la muséographie, l'archéologie et les langues indiennes, la géographie humaine, la création littéraire, les techniques artistiques et littéraires, l'art dramatique, la civilisation byzantine, la civilisation arabe et islamique, les civilisations asiatiques: chinoise, hindoue, japonaise, la littérature africaine d'expression anglaise ou française, la littérature du Commonwealth. Je m'en voudrais de no point mentionner aussi les études centrées sur un pays ou sur un continent, comme celles qui sont consacrées à la Russie, aux États-Unis, à l'Amérique latine, à l'Afrique, à l'Asie, au Commonwealth; ces centres d'études regionales sont ordinairement subventionnés soit par des Fondations philanthropiques soit par notre ministère des Affaires extérieures.[18]

Les humanités, qu'elles soient anciennes ou modernes, sont des *studia humanitatis*, c'est-à-dire ne doivent jamais perdre de vue l'homme mais rester des études de tout ce qu'il y a de plus essentiellement humain; elles comprennent, comme le mot l'indique, un ensemble d'études plus humaines, *humaniores disciplinae*; elles enseignent, tel est leur objet fondamental, le culte de l'homme et de ce qui est humain sous le mode universel. Pas seulement sous un mode local, ou régional, ou provincial ou national. Mais par suite de l'accroissement phénoménal du savoir, faute de quoi il n'existe point cependant de véritable culture de l'esprit, et de la prolifération des connaissances spéciales appliquées à une discipline particulière, on consacre hélas! un peu partout de moins en moins d'énergie et de temps aux études littéraires proprement dites; celles-ci s'amenuisent comme une peau de chagrin dans les écoles secondaires et les collèges.

Or, le savoir ne suffit pas; l'acquisition des connaissances précises et scientifiques ne suffit pas, si l'on veut être un humaniste, un homme cultivé; il faut aussi étudier l'homme et ses oeuvres, la personne humaine et ses multiples aspects; il faut enfin s'initier à l'art de sentir et de vouloir. Telle est l'essence même, la signification profonde de l'humanisme. Le nouvel humanisme, l'humanisme du XXe siècle qui est en train de se forger sous notre regard de façon tout à fait indépendante de l'humanisme gréco-latin de l'Antiquité et de la Renaissance, se doit de garder ce trait distinctif et, pour cette raison, de maintenir les études littéraires. Les humanités modernes du XXe siècle qui n'accordent point une place importante aux études littéraires sont une parodie du véritable humanisme, une piperie de mots, une trahison; à vrai dire, elles en sont une contrefaçon, un succédané, un ersatz; ma conviction intime est qu'elles seront dans l'avenir aussi capricieuses, changeantes et variées que la mode. C'est que les partisans de ces humanités sont portés à confrondre la notion de moderne avec celle du temps et du temps actuel. Ainsi Homère a beau avoir écrit l'*Iliade* et l'*Odyssée*, il y a plus de trente siècles, il est encore très moderne dans ses peintures et ses portraits de l'homme et de la femme, de la guerre et de la paix, de la vie et de la mort, de la barbarie et de la civilisation; il y a chez lui un je ne sais quoi de fraternel et d'humain qui l'apparente à nous, de sorte qu'il me paraît moins vieux que le journal d'hier, lequel est souvent illisible.

Les études canadiennes[19] se sont taillé progressivement, surtout depuis 1950, une place enviable dans l'enseignement au Canada. Par là j'entends tout particulièrement les disciplines suivantes:[20] l'histoire du Canada, la littérature orale, le folklore, l'archivistique, la muséographie, l'histoire du droit, de l'Église, de la musique, des beaux-arts, de l'enseignement, de la constitution, du droit canon, les institutions, la civilisation, les arts, et les lettres. Enfin les Canadiens montrent plus d'amour-propre que par le passé, sont de plus en plus conscients de leur identité et de leur nationalité. Témoin l'expansion de notre littérature qui est aujourd'hui enseignée outre-frontière, notamment en plusieurs universités, des États-Unis, de Grande-Bretagne, de France, et du Commonwealth. Témoin aussi la *Literary History of Canada,*[21] le *Dictionnaire Biographique Canadien,* le *Dictionnaire des Oeuvres Littéraires du Québec,* le *Dictionnaire Canadien,* etc., autant de productions qui révèlent une activité linguistique et littéraire, historique et scientifique de bon aloi.

L'état présent des humanités dans l'enseignement au Canada pose nombre de problèmes et soulève plus d'une question. Quelle est la véritable signification de l'humanisme aujourd'hui? Quel est le rôle de l'humanisme dans la création de la culture à venir? N'y aurait-il pas des humanités sans valeurs? Quelles sont à l'heure actuelle les valeurs humanistiques? Quel rapport y a-t-il entre la formation humaniste et la religion? L'écran de cinéma et de télévision ne pourrait-il pas servir à l'expression des valeurs des humanités?

Les humanités seront à jamais d'actualité ou pertinentes parce qu'elles sont les arts de la communication, les arts de la continuité, les arts de la critique. Loin d'oublier l'homme, elles entretiennent le culte de l'homme et de ses oeuvres. Elles visent à rendre l'homme plus humain. *Studia humanitatis, humaniores disciplinae.*

Références

[1] Watson Kirkconnell and A.S.P. Woodhouse, *The Humanities in Canada* (Ottawa: Humanities Research Council of Canada, 1947).

[2] F. E. L. Priestley, *The Humanities in Canada* (A report prepared for the Humanities Research Council of Canada) (Toronto: University of Toronto Press, 1964).

[3] R. M. Wiles, *The Humanities in Canada* (Toronto: University of Toronto, Press, 1966). R. M. Wiles a aussi préparé, pour le Conseil Canadien de recherche en humanités, les publications suivantes: *Scholarly Reporting in the Humanities* (4e impression), *Inventory of Research in Progress* (1971, 1972), *Canadian Directory of Scholars in the Humanities.*

⁴ Il m'a été donné, pour avoir visité à trois reprises toutes les universités du Canada, de rencontrer des directeurs de département qui étaient loin de connaître tous les membres de leur personnel enseignant.

⁵ Aux plus récents Congrès de sociétés savantes, tenus à l'Université de Toronto au printemps de 1974, j'ai compté vingt-sept associations et quatorze sociétés, sans parler des réunions d'autres organismes. Voici la liste des vingt-sept Associations canadiennes: 1. géographes; 2. écoles de service social; 3. études latino-américaines; 4. hispanistes; 5. philosophie; 6. recherche sémiotique; 7. littérature comparée; 8. linguistique; 9. linguistique comparée; 10. études de langue et de littérature du Commonwealth; 11. littératures canadienne et québecoise; 12. études canadiennes; 13. professeurs d'allemand; 14. professeurs d'anglais; 15. professeurs de français; 16. byzantinistes; 17. sciences administratives; 18. économique; 19. études classiques; 20. professeurs de droit; 21. science politique; 22. écoles universitaires de nursing; 23. études d'Asie du Sud; 24. science statistique; 25. avancement des études néerlandaises; 26. étude de la religion; 27. recherche et éducation pour la paix.

Voici maintenant la liste des quatorze sociétés qui tinrent aussi leur congrès annuel à Toronto: 1. Société royale du Canada; 2. études asiatiques; 3. histoire et philosophie des sciences; 4. histoire de l'Église; 5. histoire de l'Église catholique du Canada; 6. histoire du droit; 7. histoire du Canada; 8. étude de l'éducation; 9. étude de l'enseignement supérieur; 10. étude comparée des civilisations; 11. étude des religions; 12. étude théologique; 13. études italiennes; 14. études bibliques. En revanche, il y a trente ans, en 1944, on pouvait compter sur les doigts des deux mains le nombre des sociétés savantes qui tenaient alors leur congrès annuel.

⁶ Voici une courte liste, forcément incomplète, des revues savantes qui sont nées depuis 1940: *Manitoba Arts Review, Journal of the Canadian Linguistic Association, Ontario History, Saskatchewan History, Cahiers des Dix, Culture, Canadian Music Journal, Canadian Journal of Theology, Canadian Review of Comparative Literature, Canadian Journal of Religious Thought, Canadian Journal of Linguistics, Histoire de l'Amérique française, Cahiers de Droit, Études françaises, Études Littéraires, Archives de Folklore, Canadian Literature, Dialogue, Phoenix, Cahier d'études anciennes, Laval Théologique et Philosophique, Art and Archaeology, Reformation and Renaissance, Studia Canonica, Mosaic, Cahiers de psychomécanique du langage, Canadian Current Law, Cahier de Géographie de Québec, Cahiers d'histoire, Diogenes, Mediaeval Studies. Études slaves et est-européennes. Studia Varia, Canadian Journal of African Studies, Canadian Journal of Philosophy, Canadian Journal of Theology, Canadian Review of American Studies, Canadian Slavic Studies, Canadian Slavonic Papers, Translatio, Études internationales,* etc.

⁷ Hélas! on rencontre aussi beaucoup d'étudiants qui, faute d'avoir étudié l'histoire à l'école secondaire et au collège, ignorent tout de l'histoire européenne et de l'histoire du Canada. Au lieu de leur enseigner l'histoire, leurs maîtres leur ont probablement appris à critiquer la société et les événements du jour, comme si l'actualité et la critique de la société pouvaient remplacer l'histoire. Les cours d'histoire devraient être obligatoires.

⁸ Nous prions le lecteur, curieux de plus ample information, de consulter, entre autres publications, le *Bulletin des Humanités gréco-latines* que publie régulièrement, depuis novembre 1970, la direction générale de l'enseignement collégial, au Ministère de l'éducation du Québec.

⁹ Le projet-pilote de l'enseignement du grec à McGill qui a déjà été adopté par plusieurs universités du pays et par plus de cinquante universités étrangères,

Ancient Greek: A Structural Programme, est l'oeuvre des professeurs C. D. Ellis et A. Schachter, de McGill, qui ont aussi bénéficié de l'aide de J. G. Griffith, Fellow and Tutor in Classics, Jesus College, Oxford. Commencé il y a une dizaine d'années, il a été depuis lors mis au point et pratiqué avec beaucoup de succès. Pour ce qui est du latin, plusieurs universités canadiennes ont adopté la méthode du *Cambridge Latin Course*. Au moment où j'écris cet essai, le *Cambridge Greek Course* n'est pas encore terminé.

[10] Ce sont deux projets en cours de réalisation à l'Université Laval, Québec.

[11] Le Centre d'études de la Renaissance, à l'Université de Sherbrooke, est beaucoup plus récent que celui, plus ancien, mieux connu, et plus actif, de l'Université de Toronto. Ce dernier publie *Renaissance and Reformation*.

[12] Pour ma part, j'ai traduit le *De transitu Hellenismi ad christianismum* (1535) de Guillaume Budé; c'est la première traduction à jamais paraitre, avec le texte français en regard (Sherbrooke: Editions Paulines, 1973).

Mon ancien élève, Guy Lavoie, vient de traduire en français toute la correspondance grecque de Guillaume Budé: celle-ci, comprenant cinquante-sept lettres, doit bientôt paraître en librairie—la première du genre—avec le texte grec en regard. Un autre ancien élève, Fernand Beaudieu, doit bientôt publier sa traduction du *De Philogia* de Budé, la première à jamais paraître avec le texte original en regard.

[13] La traduction anglaise du premier volume de la *Correspondance* d'Erasme a paru en 1974 aux Presses de l'Université de Toronto. Mon collègue, Benoît Beaulieu, vient de traduire en français le neuvième volume de la *Correspondance* d'Erasme. Les Presses de l'Université de Toronto publient régulièrement *Erasmus in English*.

[14] *The Scholemaster* de Roger Ascham a été édité par R. J. Shoeck (Toronto: Dent, 1966). Le même auteur a publié aussi *Editing Sixteenth Century Texts* (1966) et *Chaucer Criticism* (1960, 1961) en deux volumes. Il est l'un des éditeurs de *The Complete Works of St. Thomas More*.

[15] J'ai traduit—c'est la première traduction française—*An Apologie for Poetrie* (1595), avec le texte anglais en regard de la traduction (Québec: Les Presses de l'Université Laval, 1965).

[16] L'édition des *Oeuvres Complètes* de Sir Walter Raleigh a été confiée à Pierre Lefranc et John Roberts, professeurs à l'Université Laval.

[17] Ce tableau relatif aux études de la Renaissance est beaucoup trop maigre pour être complet. Je n'ai point parlé, par exemple, du retour à la musique de la Renaissance ou des rapports entre les arts et la littérature à l'époque de la Renaissance. Quoiqu'il en soit, la formation humaniste, fondée sur l'étude de l'Antiquité et de la Renaissance, reste toujours valable même au XXe siècle. En 1860, Jacob Burckhardt écrivait avec beaucoup de justesse: "Education in the classical heritage of the Greco-Roman and the Renaissance fast would provide authentic values to compensate for the failures of bourgeois commercialism and materialism." Cela est encore plus vrai aujourd'hui qu'il y a un siècle, car, par suite de l'abaissement de la culture classique et du manque de discipline classique, il est devenu extrêmement difficile d'opposer une vraie digue à l'envahissement des humanités sans valeurs que charrient, trop souvent, à longueur de journée, les divers moyens de communication sociale.

[18] Sans doute ma liste est-elle incomplète. Libre au lecteur mieux informé de la compléter à l'envi.

[19] La Fondation d'Études du Canada (252 Bloor Street West, Toronto), dont la création remonte à 1970, publie un rapport annuel et encourage une série de projets fort intéressants.

littérature cana-

déjà paru jusqu'ici,

Les Presses de

ed that she be handed ove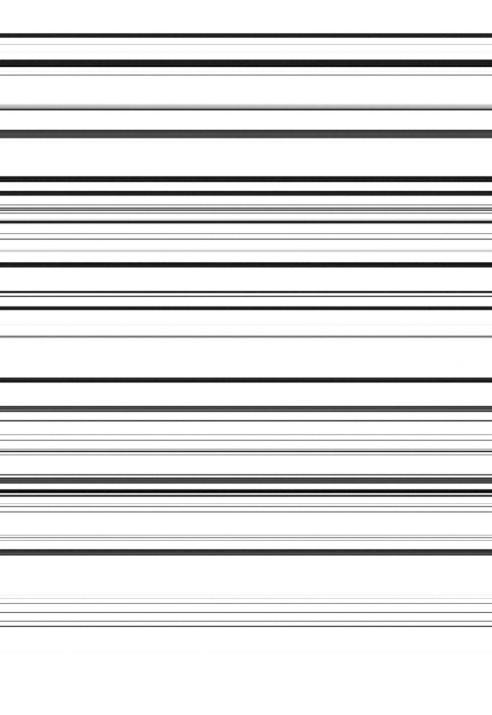
from that ignominy, sent I
African love stories were tu
lated treatments occur in
Romeo and Juliet and in
terplay of two societies, su
Red Gap.)

Following the lead set
man chroniclers, gossips,
tra legend, translating her
be freely manipulated in
Florus noted Antony's de
country, his name, his tos
blamed it on a shrewd, w
pire for her favours, trait
committed suicide only be
tavian. Dion Cassius embe
tra tested the effects of a
the fact that Octavian be
power, licentiousness, and
rous depravity that he d
Paterculus summed up he
racy: "Caesar fought for
ruin."

Cleopatra was of Gree
tarch, who integrated her
and slander, his genius tu
shame into a unified, cr
traits plunged Antony int
gree of love." Frenzy was
along by the woman as
and must go where she di

With the decline of R
symbol of Eastern decad
authors cautiously began
cent de Beauvais in *Spe*
marriage to Antony with
ing her faults, refrained
with other suiciders and
of carnal lovers, describin
luptuous. For him the C
appropriate self-damnati

[20] Plusieurs de ces disciplines, comme l'histoire du Canada et la littérature canadienne, sont enseignées aux niveaux secondaire et collégial.

[21] J'ai traduit cet ouvrage, dont trente mille exemplaires ont déjà paru jusqu'ici, sous le titre de *Histoire Littéraire du Canada* (Québec: Les Presses de l'Université Laval, 1970).

The Cleopatra Theme in World Literature up to 1700

by J. Max Patrick, D. Phil.

Pascal was not necessarily right when he claimed that if Cleopatra's nose had been longer the whole course of subsequent history would have been changed. Obviously her fascination depended on other than nasal origins. Moreover, it might well have sufficed to make mankind esteem long noses beautiful. However Shakespeare's equally famous remark, that Cleopatra had "infinite variety," though perhaps inapplicable to the real woman, is an apt description of her multiple roles in legend and literature. A proper treatment of their diversity would require several volumes. Accordingly, what follows here is but an introductory survey of the Cleopatra theme mainly as it appears in world literature before 1700. The model for it is the more thorough thematic approach made by Watson Kirkconnell in *The Celestial Cycle: The Theme of Paradise Lost* (1952), *That Invincible Samson: The Theme of* Samson Agonistes (1964), and *Awake the Courteous Echo: The Themes and Prosody of* Comus, Lycidas, *and* Paradise Regained (1973).

The historical Cleopatra was not a product of one of those Egyptian brother-sister marriages. Born with the normal number of grandparents in 69 B.C., Cleopatra VI was reared in an amoral but cultivated court. Like the Tudor Elizabeth I, she seems to have had strong features, fair skin, reddish hair, and mastery of several languages. And like the English Queen she was a shrewd, popular, somewhat machiavellian ruler, a good organizer, a defender of her people's faith, and a woman who used her charms and talents for both personal and political ends. Under her Egypt, despite Roman domination, enjoyed economic prosperity and freedom from the uprisings that imperilled previous rulers. Political reasons induced her at the age of nineteen to enter into a union with Julius Caesar, then fifty years old; and it was to protect her throne and country that, about 46 B.C. she followed him to Rome with their child, Caesarion. According her no more than political attentions, he installed her person on the far side of the Tiber and her statue in the Temple of Venus Genetrix. For, even in life, she was a symbol of the Nile's fertility. After the assassination of Caesar in 44, she hurried back to Egypt and, by pursuing a policy of friendly cooperation with Rome, prevented her country from being completely looted. It was in keeping with this policy that she married Mark Antony.

With that marriage she entered literature, for Roman propagandists against Antony made her a symbol of woman's power over man, a siren who drove men to the enslavement of frenzied love. In Epode IX and Ode I.37, Horace denounced her for sissifying generals, for reducing Antony to the effeminacy of sleeping under mosquito nets! Nevertheless he grudgingly called her *non humilis mulier*—no humble woman—thus recognizing some strength in her character. Cicero condemned her for arrogance, and Propertius castigated her as a harlot queen in his elegies. They are examples of the masculine tendency to defend male-dominated societies by portraying females as threats to "civilization." So ancient Israelites and seventeenth-century Puritans personified their perils as feminine—as the whore of Babylon; and John Knox similarly denounced government by queens as "the monstrous regiment of women." The theme was to be reiterant in treatments of Cleopatra.

Virgil attacked her obliquely in the *Aeneid*; for there was an obvious similarity between the involvement of the African Queen Dido with Aeneas, the legendary ancestor of the Romans, and the dallying of Cleopatra, another African Queen, with the Roman Antony. But Virgil had the difference in mind: Aeneas gave up his Queen and went on to do his duty, whereas Antony lingered with his, imperilling Rome. And later history provided a third instance of the themes of clashing civilizations, private love versus public interest, and east meets west: during the Second Punic War, Masinissa, a general allied with Rome, captured and fell in love with another African Queen, Sophonisba; but the Romans, fearing that her influence might be pernicious, demanded that she be handed over to them, and Masinissa, to save her from that ignominy, sent her poison, which she drank. All three African love stories were to be retold with many variations. (Related treatments occur in the theme of love versus family feud in *Romeo and Juliet* and in moving pictures that centre on the interplay of two societies, such as *Yank at Oxford* and *Ruggles at Red Gap*.)

Following the lead set by Horace, Virgil, and Propertius, Roman chroniclers, gossips, and moralizers crystallized the Cleopatra legend, translating her and her mates into symbols that could be freely manipulated in easy formulae. Thus Lucius Anneus Florus noted Antony's decline into a monster "forgetful of his country, his name, his toga, and the emblems of his office" and blamed it on a shrewd, wanton Cleopatra who demanded Empire for her favours, traitorously led the retreat at Actium, and committed suicide only because she was unable to fascinate Octavian. Dion Cassius embellished the story, alleging that Cleopatra tested the effects of asps upon her slaves. Orosius, ignoring the fact that Octavian began the war, declared that Cleopatra's power, licentiousness, and flattery so nourished Antony's amorous depravity that he declared war on his own country. And Paterculus summed up her effect with more balance than accuracy: "Caesar fought for the safety of the world; Antony, for its ruin."

Cleopatra was of Greek ancestry, and it was a Greek, Plutarch, who integrated her legend. Starting from anecdote, gossip, and slander, his genius transformed her from a mere symbol of shame into a unified, credible *femme fatale* whose bewitching traits plunged Antony into what Bacon was to call "the mad degree of love." Frenzy was his overt theme: Antony "was dragged along by the woman as if he had become incorporate with her and must go where she did."

With the decline of Rome the obligation to attack her as a symbol of Eastern decadence and rival imperialism faded, and authors cautiously began to treat her with some sympathy. Vincent de Beauvais in *Speculum Maius* (ca. 1244) described her marriage to Antony with some respect. Dante, without condoning her faults, refrained from assigning her to infernal depths with other suiciders and relegated her to the less agonizing circle of carnal lovers, describing her as "lussuriosa"—luxurious and voluptuous. For him the Cleopatra theme was that lust brings its appropriate self-damnation. In *De Casibus Virorum* (1355) and

De Claribus Mulieribus (1360), Boccaccio made her exemplify how great persons fall from eminence—in her case because of sensuality so passionate that she even enjoyed succumbing to the serpents. He also briefly introduced her into prose fiction in the tale of *The Amorous Fiametta*. When that lady's beloved went to war, she tried to convince herself that she was the most miserable of women. Comparing herself with others, she reflected that Cleopatra's love agonies always had compensations: she lost Caesar but had their child to comfort her; and when life became unendurable without Antony, she found "a wholesome medicine" in the vipers that sucked out both her blood and her life.

This Cleopatra felt affection for her child, suffered for love, had some nobility in passion, and ended her life partly for love. Thus Boccaccio partly transformed her from classical whore to medieval courtly lover.

Chaucer completed the process in *The Legend of Good Women*. Dramatically focusing on Cleopatra's death, he delineated her not as the traditional siren but as a loyal wife. He relates that a Senator named Antonius, full of ardour for his lass Cleopatra, set the world at no value and sought only to serve her. Being a courtly lady, she esteemed this worthy gentle warrior for his chivalry and married him. Manipulating history, Chaucer made Antony, not Cleopatra, initiate the flight from Actium; and after his death, this good and loyal wife erected a jewelled shrine for him, prepared a pit of serpents, and died: "Was nevere onto hire love a trewere quene." Chaucer adds a delicious touch by having her go naked into the pit of snakes.

In *Confessio Amantis*, Gower refined this detail: as in life Cleopatra was torn by love's pangs, so in dying she was ripped by serpents' fangs! For him, as for John Lydgate in *The Fall of Princes*, Cleopatra was a vehicle for moralizing. But in the anonymous *Roman de Jules César* the problem was amorous: Caesar came, saw Cleopatra, and was so conquered by love that he could not sleep. She was similarly afflicted. But negotiations brought happiness—and ended the insomnia.

The rise of printing in the Renaissance made Plutarch more available. The French translation of the *Lives* begun by Lazare de Baif and finished by George de Selve in 1543 helped to inspire Marc Antoine Meret's Neo-Latin *Caesar* in the next year. It was the play Shakespeare probably had in mind when he had Polonius boast of acting Caesar "once i' th' university." Certainly it is full of Polonian platitudes. But its heroine was Calpurnia.

The favourite heroines in early Renaissance drama (as distinguished from medieval) were Sophonisba, Dido, and Cleopatra. The first of these African Qeeens led the way in a loosely constructed play by Careotto and a regular classical one by Trissino. The second was the heroine of *Didone*, by Giambattista Giraldi Cintio, and it so delighted the Duke of Ferrara that he commissioned Cintio to compose *Cleopatra Tragedia*, which was acted in 1543 though not published until forty years later. Accordingly it ranks as the first of over two dozen plays on Cleopatra (not to mention operas) that were written by European authors before 1700. Its theme, that heroic death cancels earlier mistakes, was ably developed in a panoramic treatment of the kind later used by Shakespeare.

Giraldi Cintio relied chiefly on Plutarch. But scholars have strangely overlooked the prose compendium that was used by several of the authors of Cleopatra plays who followed him. *La Vita di Cleopatra*, composed in 1551 by Giulio Landi, was based on a careful combing of most of the classical sources. Deploring her fault of pride, Landi nevertheless had some admiration for her, and he depicts her as enterprising, calculating, and ambitious but neither vicious nor lascivious. His volume seems to have inspired both Cesare de' Cesari's Italian *Cleopatra Tragedia* and Etienne Jodelle's French *Cléopâtre Captive* in the next year. (Alessandro Spinello's *Cleopatra Tragedia*, acted in 1550, had a heroine unidentifiable with the famous Queen.)

In his plays on Dido and Cleopatra, Giraldi Cintio established the pattern of the Repentant Heroine that was developed by de' Cesari and Jodelle. Their Cleopatras lament incessantly, expounding the themes that passion does not pay, the world is not well lost for love, duty to country must prevail over the selfish extremes of love, and their complement, that prolonged agonized repentance and heroic death may bring salvation. Both of these authors began with Antony's death—though he appears as a ghost—and ended a few hour's later with Cleopatra's suicide. This overconcern for unity of time minimizes the action so that the plays are little more than elegies, lyric rather than dramatic in tone. They are a curious blend of Neo-Senecanism, obedience to what were thought to be classical rules for drama, and the medieval *De Casibus* tradition. They were part of an international movement of authors who wrote in the same vein—Celso Pistorelli in *Marc' Antonio e Cleopatra*, an Italian tragedy produced in 1576; Robert Garnier in *Marc Antoine* (1578) and the English redaction from French made of it by the Countess of Pembroke in the *Tragedie of*

Antonie (1592); Samuel Daniel in *The Tragedie of Cleopatra* (1594), which he composed as a sequel to the Countess's drama; and Nicholas Montreux in *La Tragédie de Cléopâtre* (1594). These authors were less interested in drama as it is now conceived than in reactions to pathetic circumstances and in states of mind. Their works are intended for contemplation and the upholding of awful examples of the personal and national ruin consequent upon rulers putting self-indulgence above duty. Garnier's Cleopatra is overwhelmed with woe because of the damage she did her country; as a result, she is quite static. But she is even flatter in the Pembroke redaction, for the Countess took care to remove all glamour from her. Sarah Fielding was also harsh in her *Lives of Cleopatra and Octavia*, published in 1757; but on so slight a basis it would be unfair to generalize that authoresses see Cleopatra with the jaundiced eye of jealousy.

The extensive revisions that Samuel Daniel made to his sequel to the Countess of Pembroke's *Antonie* reveal that he reacted against her meanness to Cleopatra and against representing the Queen as abject, overlamenting, and unspirited in defeat. In his ultimate portrayal Daniel describes her as crushed in body but not in spirit and as healthy in repentance; thus her passion becomes heroic devotion and her pride becomes dignity. In sometimes vibrant poetry he began to recognize the dramatic possibilities of the tension themes that were developed later—love versus honour, passion versus duty, maternal affection versus royal obligations, and patriotism versus selfishness.

Meanwhile the interest of playwrights in Cleopatra extended beyond Italy, France, and England. About 1555 the Portuguese Sa de Miranda devoted a tragedy to her, but less than twelve lines of it are extant. They suggest that his approach was like that of de' Cesari, Jodelle, Garnier, Daniel, and Montreux. But it was otherwise in Germany where Hans Sachs first damned Cleopatra in 1538 in a crude poem, *Historia von Dreyen Heidnischen... Frawen*, relisted her wickednesses in a monologue, *Die Zwölff Argen Königen* (1562), and gave slightly more favourable treatment to her and Antony in 1560. Written in ding-dong metre and based on German translations of Plutarch and Boccaccio, this seven-act tragedy reminds one of what Shakespeare's Cleopatra told Anthony:

> The quick comedians
> Extemporally will state us, and present
> Our Alexandrian revels: Anthony
> Shall be brought drunken forth, and I shall see

Some squeaking Cleopatra boy my greatness
I' th' posture of a whore.

However, educated Englishmen did not think of Cleopatra in
this manner. The similarities between the Queen who was the last
of the Ptolemies and Elizabeth I, the last of the Tudors, was not
overlooked. Daniel's play was probably a warning to Elizabeth
that pride and passion (that is, her affair with Essex) could lead a
country to ruin. John Heywood in his *History of Women* called
Elizabeth "a Cleopatra for her bounty." And Fulke Greville
destroyed his play, *Antony and Cleopatra*, out of fear that some
might find in it a parallel between the falls of Antony and Essex.

It is probable that Greville, like his predecessors since Giraldi
Cintio, tried to obey the dramatic unities of time, place, and
action. However, Sachs made no such attempt and Spain provides
another exception, *Marco Antonio y Cleopatra*, a tragedy written
about 1582 by Diego Lopez de Castro. Devoting his first two acts
to Antony's philandering with an infatuated woman named Mar-
cela, de Castro demonstrates that the Roman was already well on
the road to ruin before he went to Egypt and met Cleopatra, thus
partly exonerating her from blame.

But it was Shakespeare who recognized that it is less important
for a playwright to resolve issues, simplify characters, and draw
morals than to dramatize them. Indeed, there is no need to expatiate on his superiority; copiousness in treatment, complexity of
characterization, exploitation of a cosmic panorama, and richness
of poetry constitute only part of that excellence. Notable also is
the distinctive and functional dualism of his Antony and his Cleopatra. They live on two levels of experience, the legendary and the
actual. Aware that they are creating a legend, they are humanly
aware of the strain of living up to it: "Here I am Antony / Yet
cannot hold this visible shape," he declares. And Caesar says to
him, "You are the word for war," thus recognizing that Antony is
a type beyond himself. So Cleopatra declares, "My Oblivion is a
very Antony." And in the birthday scene there is a rapid alterna-
tion between their ideal roles and actual selves: when he suddenly
ceases to be natural and puts on the legendary, she comments,
"Since my Lord is Antony, I will be Cleopatra." These alterna-
tions and the double images thus created are keys to the extraordinary vividness and realism of their characterization.

Shakespeare's excellence did not stem the tide of works about
Cleopatra or confine them to drama. Indeed, she had already been

treated variously: in 1572, by Guillaume Belliard in *Les Merveilleuses Amours de . . . Antoine et de Cléopâtre*; touched upon by Lope de Vega's *Los Triumphos de Octaviano*, about 1603; and more fully considered, in German, by A. Olearius Adonis in his *Historia von der Cleopatra* (1606). And following Shakespeare, writings about her multiplied. Hans Thomissen Stege approached her first in Danish with *Cleopatra, en Historisk Tragoedia* and then in Neo-Latin with *Cleopatra Carmine Descripta*, both in 1609; and 1624 saw a Dutch tragedy, *Anthonius en Cleopatra*, by Wilhelmus van Nieuvelandt.

In general, seventeenth-century treatments of Cleopatra tended toward increasing experiment and imaginative licence. In *The False One* (1609) John Fletcher and Philip Massinger explored her relations with Caesar, but unlike Bernard Shaw in his far later *Caesar and Cleopatra*, they saw in her not the undeveloped freshness of youth but rather an experienced courtesan with a heroic soul. Recognizing each others' innate nobility when they first met, she and Caesar knew exalted love. But when he was dazzled by Egypt's wealth, she spurned him for having the soul of a tradesman. Then, when his valour in battle proved her wrong, their love blossomed. The theme of this forerunner of heroic drama is, accordingly, that heroism is the supreme value.

In 1626 Thomas May succeeded in differentiating his *Tragedie of Cleopatra* by ransacking the classics for colourful details which he grafted on the story in such a hodgepodge that his heroine's variety contradicted itself. Nine years later Jean de Mairet's *Marc Antoine, ou la Cléopâtre* achieved novelty by partly reversing the roles so that Antony became changeable and almost coquettish, and Cleopatra became a Constantia, unvaryingly loyal and devoted to him. Mairet's focus was on Antony, but in the same year his rival, Isaac de Benserade, balanced this by centring *La Cléopâtre* on the heroine. His earthy, selfish, clever Cleopatra dominates over Antony and is inconsiderate of his self respect. After his death, she tries to outwit the cold, calculating Augustus, but he wisely refuses to meet her eyes. She illustrates the theme that politics and power corrupt. And in 1638 Charles Chaulmer went to extremes in search of novelty. He invents a passionate love affair for Cleopatra before she meets Caesar, develops a sensational struggle with a rival, and creates a tragicomic romance of adventure in which she loses her true identity.

Meanwhile Cleopatra was treated in various works of prose and poetry. She had a brief role in the Latin and English continuations

71

of Lucan's *Pharsalia* by Thomas May (1630): they are high in literary merit. Girolamo Gratiano's full-length epic, *La Cleopatra, Poema* (1632) also deserves to be better known, though its portrayal of Cleopatra reflects the harshness of the early Roman authors. Alonso de Castillo Solórzano's *Historia de Marco y Cleopatra* (1639) is a conventional prose compilation; but it is studded by fascinatingly varied poems from Lope de Vega and other major writers. Solórzano sums up their general theme: "Goza de immunidades la hermosura," a line that a Dorothy Parker imitator might render as "Beauty brings immunity / To make love with impunity." A final judgment appears in a sonnet on Cleopatra's death by Luys de Villanova: "Love will judge her; time will pardon her."

The progress of judicious historiography is manifest in *Di Cleopatra . . . La Vita Considerata*, a scientific examination of her career published by Paganio Gaudenzio, a Swiss Italian, in 1642. It was probably used as a source by Pierre Corneille for his *La Mort de Pompée* (1643). In that play, a Cleopatra who is colder and more self-possessed than her predecessors is a heroic Queen who stands up to insolent ministers and dominates over a cringing Ptolemy. She exemplifies the theme that ambition is the sole passion worthy of a princess.

Such exaltation of Cleopatra into a heroic figure conduced to comic reactions. In 1647 John Cleveland published two trivial erotic poems, "Mark Antony" and "The Author's Mock Song to Mark Antony." The latter describes a wanton love affair with a contrasting refrain: "Never Mark Antony / Dallied more wantonly / with the fair Egyptian Queen." In 1658 William Davenant descended to cruder depths with a scene he included in a hodgepodge of short plays entitled *The Play-House to be Lett*. His Cleopatra alternately flirts with Caesar and her beloved "Tony," and engages in a fishwife-quarrel with Octavia, after which the actors shift amiably to the nearest tavern!

In contrast, *Los Aspides de Cleopatra* (Cleopatra's Asps) by Francisco de Rojas Zorilla (1645) is brilliant, sophisticated, and exquisitely formulated, especially if, contrary to scholarly tradition, it is regarded as mock heroic, as a delicious satire against the heroic mode and the artificialities of Benserade, Mairet, and Corneille. His Antony is a heroic superman, supreme in the desirable extremes of valour and virtue and well aware that the other extreme—love—is vicious, ever to be shunned. Cleopatra is a similar paragon, such a chaste, heroic Queen that she has outlawed copulation throughout Egypt, much to the annoyance of a female

72

citizen who voices objections. Their essence, freely rendered into English is as follows: "Birds and fishes do it / Rabbits never rue it. / Why can't I pursue it?" Scorning praise for her beauty and demanding honour for her valour, Cleopatra ignores such pleas and ruthlessly sentences an adultress to death by asp stings. Enter Antony—shouting his own name from a distance; and Cleopatra, previously undaunted by man or beast, feels tremors at the sound. Despising to conquer him other than by valour, she veils her face and they interchange vaunts about their intrepidity. Bold Antony challenges her to unveil her face, confident that he can resist it. But when she does, to their shamed dismay, they fall desperately in love and her dilemma is agonizing: if she marries him, her own edict will require her death; if she doesn't, she'll die for love. And he is in a like quandary, for if he returns to his wife, whom he merely likes, he will die in tepid fire. "I don't know what to do among such precise dangers," he laments. But how they solved their problems is hardly relevant here: Rojas Zorilla had trespassed beyond the Cleopatras of legend and history into fantasy.

Giovanni Delfino in *Cleopatra Tragedia* (1660) and Daniel Caspar von Lohenstein in *Cleopatra Trauer-Spiel* (1661) also trespassed, but with more verisimilitude. The Italian's play centres on an imaginary encounter between Cleopatra and Augustus in which they truly but only momentarily fall in love. Circumstances are such that their mutual suspicions prevent their love from blossoming. It may be regretted that Delfino underrealized these dramatic possibilities. (The theme, that fate may tragically make love impossible, is one that Andrew Marvell treated in the same period, though briefly, in his "My Unfortunate Lover" and "The Definition of Love.")

If Delfino underrealized the possibilities of a Cleopatra theme, Caspar von Lohenstein overdeveloped them. With encyclopaedic gusto he lards his baroque pageant-drama with erudite footnotes, and he exceeds his predecessors in richness of imagery and diction. The tendency toward heightened characterization which Montreux began and Chaulmer made sensational is extended by Lohenstein to something like Shakespeare's cosmic range but without subtlety. At the end of each act, the pagan gods generalize about the action and its significance, thus adding philosophical discussions to the elaborate spectacles. Lohenstein amazingly involves within his enormously long play nearly all the disparate tendencies in earlier Cleopatra dramas. Into a baroque pot he pours the pedantic, the sensational, the intense, the melodramatic, the cosmic, the intense,

73

the grandiose, the didactic, and the spectacular, dissolving them in the supersaturated alcohol of elaborate conceits and lush diction. His heroine is the most machiavellian of Cleopatras, and his theme is the grand doublecross. Cleopatra exploits Antony's genuine love for her to prevent him from coming to terms with Augustus. When the latter professes love for her, she agrees to kill Antony and marry Augustus. In an elaborate scene she dons bridal clothes in readiness for the bridegroom Death and drinks what she falsely claims to be poison. This leads Antony to suicide. But Augustus then refuses marriage unless she first comes to Rome, thus revealing that he wants her merely for a triumph. So she kills herself properly.

Though the English produced nothing on the scale of Lohenstein's spectacle, their interest in Cleopatra continued. Corneille's *La Mort de Pompée*, translated by the Matchless Orinda, Katherine Philips, was published as *Pompey: A Tragedy* in 1663 and found favour in repeated performances and many editions, despite a rival version, *Pompey the Great*, prepared by Waller, Godolphin, Filmer, Dorset, and Sir Charles Sedley (1664). This inspired Sedley to compose his own tragedy, *Antony and Cleopatra*, in 1667. Its complex plot, which begins after the defeat at Actium, is overloaded with facts though rich in unrealized dramatic possibilities. It centres on a rather conventional heroine's illicit passion for an ineffectual, cowardly hero. Perhaps aware of its deficiencies in poetry, noble passion, and ethical import, Sedley began to recast it as a classical tragedy with a chorus after every act. This incomplete version was published in 1702 as *Beauty the Conqueror*.

The first printing of Sedley's drama coincided with the presentation in 1677 of Dryden's masterpiece *All for Love, or the World Well Lost*. Its theme is too obvious to call for comment here other than to draw attention to the good sense with which Dryden avoided the extremes of his contemporary playwrights, the skill with which he departed from history in the confrontation of Cleopatra and Octavia, and the apt effectiveness with which he resolves the final conflicts by having Cleopatra declare that she had not been a Roman's wife without learning how to die.

In 1682 Jean de la Chapelle treated the same final phase of Antony and Cleopatra but endowed them with more warmth so that his *Cléopâtre* puts less emphasis on a love-honour conflict than on genuine love struggling with human frailties and the suspicions created by politics. After the extremes of intense characterization pushed by previous dramatists, it is pleasant to be introduced to an Antony and a Cleopatra who are credible, likeable, and sympathetic. However, Charles Champmeslé, deeming her insufficiently heroic, parodied her in *Ragotin* (1684).

Convenience alone dictates that this survey should end with the seventeenth century, for works about Cleopatra continued to pour forth, so many that only a sampling may be mentioned: Colley Cibber's *Caesar in Egypt* (1725), *Cléopâtre* by Robert Boistel (1741), Vittorio Alfieri's *Antonio e Cleopatra* (1775), *La Cleopatra Regina di Egitto* by Antonio Bonucci (1789), *Kleopatra und Antonius* by Cornelius von Ayrenhoff(1783), *Cleopatra, eine Tragödie* by August von Kotzebue (published in 1841), and *Cléopâtre* by Madame Emile de Girardin (1847). Later in the nineteenth century Landor and Tennyson wrote poems about her, transforming her into a classical, dignified, almost austere lover. But Gautier made her a *femme fatale* in an exotic background, a siren who kills the only man she loved. Wilde, Swinburne, and Pushkin similarly tore her out of history and made her a symbol of man's destructive passion and death urge. They make Cleopatra symbolize an imaginary Egypt that consumes all other cultures in the timelessness of its monuments, and their theme is that life is well lost for irresistible lust. And she recurs in well over a thousand twentieth-century treatments.

Cleopatra thus became in extremes what from the beginning she had tended to be—a composite of opposites and contradictions, impure and yet pure in love that was both heaven and hell. In real life an efficient ruler, she was transformed into a siren-strumpet in Roman legend, exalted into a symbol of lust by Dante and into a martyr for love by Chaucer. Though intended as a vehicle for moralizing by the Neo-Senecan dramatists of the Renaissance, she grew into a splendid figure of repentance under Daniel's pen. Shakespeare endowed her with infinite variety, and even Fletcher and Massinger discovered in her final stages a nobility and honour that eclipsed the faults of her past. And so she continued to develop in literature until goodness and sin, greatness and pettiness, capriciousness and steadfastness were all rolled up in one carpet with her. She became a symbol of mystery like Mona Lisa, of exotic power like the Sphinx. Combining the coquettish and the majestic, the transient and the eternal, she became what Heine, not without reason, called "the Goddess of Life."

However, a few academic observations may be in order. The literature about Cleopatra could be explored to discover what is characteristic in national literatures and what transcends them.

Certainly much fertile research remains untilled. Between 1478 and 1697 over forty plays about Cleopatra were written in ten languages, some of them unmentioned here; and at least fifteen of these have been neglected by scholars. There were also at least fifteen operas about her during that period, as well as two epics, fourteen prose accounts, and a host of minor poems. This survey has suggested how all this material is open to revealing thematic treatments, especially the significance of the related works on those other African Queens, Dido and Sophonisba. Moreover, relatively little has been written on the Cleopatra theme, and most of it is preliminary in nature: there are two dissertations by G. H. Moeller (Ulm, 1888 and Schweinfurt, 1907), that cover tragedies in Romance and Teutonic languages; another by W. Traub (Würzburg, 1938) that cursorily examines works in English; a Bonn dissertation on the Antony-Cleopatra motif in German literature (1930) by S. Vranckens; a useful but not always reliable consideration by Furness in the New Variorum edition of Shakespeare's *Antony and Cleopatra* (1907); and a somewhat gushing popularized survey, *Cleopatra in the Tide of Time*, by Oliver C. de C. Ellis, published for the Poetry Lovers Fellowship in 1947. But all of these works are sadly incomplete: for example, they make no mention of what Spaniards wrote on the theme. And they are unaware that the Library of Congress contains over a hundred unpublished theatrical pieces on Cleopatra as a consequence of a nineteenth-century law that granted copyrights when such works were filed in manuscript.

[Because of limitations of space, I have not provided proper footnotes and bibliographies for this survey: they would at least quadruple its length. However, I have three long-range projects in progress: a comprehensive bibliography of works on and related to Cleopatra; an anthology of the most significant treatments of her; and a study of the Cleopatra theme in world literature that will run to at least two volumes. Because the source material on her is vast, is not to be found comprehensively even in the largest research libraries, and requires what I lack—the linguistic proficiency of a Watson Kirkconnell—none of these projects will reach publication for at least a decade. JMP.]

The Changing Aspect of Clio

by E. Togo Salmon, F.R.S.C., F.B.A.

The eminence that the scholar honoured in this volume has attained in English studies must not be allowed to obscure his distinction in other branches of learning. Dr. Kirkconnell's first university degree was in Classics, and the wealth of references to Greek and Latin literature in his latest book shows that he still reads with pleasure the languages of ancient Athens and Rome. A paper on some aspect of the Classics should, therefore, not be out of place in the present volume; and if recent developments in Roman historiography have been chosen for the theme, it is because the ethnic material they encompass and the analogues they suggest cannot fail to interest the author of *Canada, Europe and Hitler* and the *Quellenforscher* of Milton.

It should go without saying that today's accounts of Roman history are bound to be unlike those produced in the nineteenth century. Every generation tends to view the past in the light of its own experiences, interests, and preoccupations, so that the problems of an earlier age on which historians focus their attention are always likely to be the topical ones of their own day. This certainly accounts for some of the shifts of emphasis in Roman historical studies since 1900. Today's historians are much more concerned with the economic, social, and cultural aspects of the Roman world and less with its political struggles than their predecessors, although it is interesting and instructive to note the increased attention now being paid to the political infighting in ancient Rome and its concomitant violence.

Yet one wonders whether the change that has come over Roman history since 1900 does not go far beyond the differences that might have been confidently expected in two histories of the same subject written by different generations. At any rate, it is certainly startling.

When Watson Kirkconnell won the medal for Classics at Queen's in 1916, scepticism concerning the traditional account of early Roman history, as handed down by Livy, Dionysius of Halicarnassus, and the ancient authors generally, was universal. The views disseminated by Niebuhr and his followers were endorsed by scholars everywhere throughout the nineteenth century and the first quarter of the twentieth. Not only was Livy's picture of early Rome dismissed as a romantic fairy-tale, but even the possibility of a more reliable one ever emerging was decried as a futile fantasy. To such depths had opinion of the surviving sources fallen.

The hypercriticism reached its apogee in the *Storia di Roma* of Ettore Pais, a work that perhaps appropriately coincided with the *fin de siècle*: it was published in 1898/1899, and it appeared to regard early Roman "history" as little more than a collection of old wives' tales. The new century, it is true, brought with it some reaction against Pais's aggressively negative approach. In 1907 Gaetano De Sanctis inveighed against his fellow countryman and presented an exceptionally well balanced and much more judicious account in his *Storia dei Romani*; and Pais himself, in the works he published after 1900, retreated somewhat from his earlier extremism: his five-volume *Storia di Roma* of 1928 is longer, but also more restrained than its homonymous, two-volume predecessor of thirty years earlier. Nevertheless a highly critical attitude towards the received accounts of early Roman history was still the norm until well after World War I: Beloch's *Römische Geschichte bis zum Beginn der punischen Kriege*, invariably critical and sometimes gratuitously sceptical of the ancient literary sources, appeared in 1926.

Far otherwise is it today. A chastened generation of scholars, just as learned but possibly less arrogant than their grandfathers, has gone back to the ancient writers in the belief that they provide something more than a concoction of national legends and literary anecdotes. They supply a body of factual data to supplement the bare bones of the consular *Fasti* (and today the *Fasti* are considered to be basically trustworthy and fundamental to any study of the history of Rome before the birth of Christ).

This revived faith in the ancients' version of events began manifesting itself in the seventh volume of the *Cambridge Ancient History*, which came off the press just two years after Beloch's iconoclastic opus; and, ever since, it has attracted new adherents whose confidence increases with their numbers. Today's crop of Roman historians will seem amazingly conservative to anyone who compares them with their forerunners of three quarters of a century ago, great though their indebtedness to those illustrious old masters patently is.

The extraordinary *volte-face* is not due to some shift of fashion, or to the proverbial swing of the pendulum, or even to intellectual legerdemain. The real impetus comes from the archaeologists. The discovery of Mycenaean artefacts in many parts of Italy establishes a possible basis of fact for the story that some heroes, Ulysses, say, or Diomede, wandered into Italy after the destruction of Troy. Early contacts with the Greek world are also implied by the tales about Evander, Demaratus, and others, and these receive some confirmation from the presence of sixth century Attic Pottery among the finds excavated around the church of Sant'Omobono at the southern tip of the Capitol hill. Fifth century terracotta figurines, coming to light at Rome's near neighbour Veii and showing Aeneas carrying his father Anchises to safety, suggest that Vergil's story of a Roman nation whose origins went back to refugees from Troy does not simply derive as was once believed, from a hellenophobia bred of the Pyrrhic War in the third century. Not that this means that Trojan exiles actually founded the city of Rome: the ancients themselves did not believe that. But they did believe that the city was founded on the Palatine hill about the middle of the eighth century B.C.; and shortly after World War II excavations at the northwest corner of that hill triumphantly unearthed a hut village of precisely that date at the very spot where, according to Roman tradition, Romulus had had his habitation. This, it is true, does not necessarily make Romulus an historical figure, although today there are reputable scholars ready to believe that he was a real person and not just some imaginary figment or aetiological fiction. His six successors, the kings of Rome, who until recently were usually treated as legendary, have, of course, been unequivocally rehabilitated as authentic figures of history. Moreover the last three of them probably did constitute an immigrant Etruscan dynasty, as tradition insisted, since Etruscan inscriptions have now at long last been found inside the *pomerium* and even on the Capitol itself. One member of the dynasty may even at one time have been called Caelius Vibenna, as the antiquarian emperor Claudius said he was, since that name actually occurs on an inscription securely dated to the fifth century.

There was never, of course, any very serious doubt that there was a Roman Monarchy and that it was forced to make way for the Roman Republic. But the traditional date for the expulsion of the kings, about 500 B.C., has been frequently questioned: Beloch appeared ready to put it as late as the fourth century. Today's belief is that it happened more or less when Livy said it did. At any rate, recent excavations in the Roman *forum* have turned up evidence in the building known as the *regia* to support that date.

The tales told about the youthful Republic may also have some basis of fact. True, the intervention of Castor and Pollux at the Battle of Lake Regillus shortly after 500 remains as mythical as ever; but it is not straining credulity unduly to believe that the early Republic did worship those divine heroes and build a temple for them, for they are named in archaic Latin in a dedicatory inscription of approximately that date recently found at a short distance from Rome.

None of the newly discovered material places the traditional account of early Rome securely beyond cavil or reproach. It provides circumstantial corroboration rather than positive proof. But the significant thing is that the new evidence all tends in the same direction. Archaeological finds casting doubt on the old stories have seldom, if ever, occurred, and it is this steady and constant accumulation of confirmatory testimony that has brought scholars back to Livy. No one thinks that every detail of his version describes exactly what happened (to quote Ranke's famous dictum about the optimum nature of history), but it is now generally agreed that, overall, his picture is essentially trustworthy. Many uncertainties still remain: but then Livy himself, like Cicero before him, was well aware that there had been falsification of the annals of early Rome.

The archaeology that has illuminated so much is very different from the archaeology of an earlier day. Already by the second half of the nineteenth century archaeology had ceased to be the reckless, ruthless, and rapacious scramble for buried artistic loot that it had been a hundred years earlier. A growing realization of the valuable contribution it might make to knowledge and understanding of the past led gradually to its development into a true science, and what had begun as a hunt for masterpieces of sculpture, painting, or pottery became a conscientious search for scraps of evidence, of whatever kind and of whatever artistic worth.

This has engendered a much livelier and truer appreciation of the non-Roman character of most of early Italy. The diversity of its many different peoples and the reciprocal nature of their relations with Rome are now far better known and more accurately assessed. Long before the nineteenth century ended the *objets d'art*, many of them Greek but some of them indigenous, disgorged in fantastic quantity by the tombs of Etruria, had caused the importance of Greeks and Etruscans in pre-Roman Italy to be well realized and even taken for granted. It remained for the twentieth century, for scholars like Nissen in 1901 or Devoto in the nineteen thirties, to rescue the other inhabitants of early Italy from the near oblivion of their centuries-old obscurity. The involvement of these Italic peoples with the Roman Republic made it an urgent matter to find out more about them if the history of the Republic was ever to be properly understood.

It is now clear that von Duhn's somewhat schematic picture of a prehistoric Italy invaded successively by interring and incinerating peoples, whose descendants had ultimately settled down with the "Rome-Rimini" line as their mutual boundary (the cremators to the west of it and the inhumers to the east), is greatly oversimplified. The peoples of protohistoric Italy were more jumbled than that. Even the postulated invasions have been called into question: theories of "infiltration" and "indigenism," of "formation" as distinct from "derivation," have been advanced.

This affects one's view of the Etruscans *inter alios*. The old conception of them as immigrants from overseas, who brought with them their own fully developed national consciousness and advanced material culture, has been discarded. Not that this solves the "mystery" of the Etruscans by any means. But it does ventilate the possibility that, whatever their ethnic components, it was on Italian soil that they grew up into a nation. Even their language, undeciphered though it remains, has become less baffling with the discovery at Caeretan Pyrgi in 1964 of the golden pseudo-bilinguals, in Punic and Etruscan.

The Etruscans, however, were only one of the non-Roman peoples to clash with the Roman Republic. There were also Apuli, Lucani, Marsi, Samnites, Umbri, and Vestini, to name only a few; and all have recently come under intense scrutiny. The approach to the history of the Roman Republic has been transformed in consequence. Today that history is no longer written as if it dealt only with the Romans and occasionally with some Greeks and Etruscans. Agrarian legislation and the Gracchi can no longer be discussed in an almost exclusively Roman context: the impact and effect on the disparate and heterogeneous peoples of non-Roman Italy have to be taken into consideration. Illustrative of the new trend is Toynbee's monumental *Hannibal's Legacy*, which appeared in 1965 and conscientiously seeks to explore every corner of the polyglot Saturnian land; and there have been other writers too with much to say about the Latin and Italian "allies" of Rome. The heart of von Wilamowitz-Moellendorf, who called for studies of this sort as long ago as 1915, would certainly rejoice.

The upshot has been emphatic vindication of Vergil: assuredly it *was* an immense task to establish the Roman nation. He, like other ancient writers (apart from Cato), chose to display his antiquarian knowledge of early Italy by allusion rather than by systematic exposition. Thus, about many matters we had only vague hints or casual statements torn from their original contexts. Long ignored, if not categorically rejected as merely fanciful, these stray gobbets of information now acquire significance. The philology of Messapic inscriptions and the chance discovery (since 1970) of hundreds of large incised *stelae* on the "spur" of the Italian "boot" suggest that the scattered notices of Illyrian penetration into Italy have some basis in fact. Cato's statement that Capua in Campania was founded by Etruscans about 800 B.C. seems substantiated by Villanovan burials recently uncovered there. Perhaps it is not over-optimistic to suggest that modern research will make good the non-survival of Cato's *Origines* in other respects also.

All of this means that today's historian must seek to assign to the city of Rome its true proportions in the context of all Italy, putting emphasis not only on Roman policy but also on local conditions in the areas where it was being carried out.

The picture of Rome's relations with nations outside Italy may not have been revolutionized to quite the same extent; but it, too, is being filled out. Careful research, archaeological as well as historical, has made Carthage and the Hellenistic kingdoms of the eastern Mediterranean much better known than they were fifty years ago, and the veil of obscurity surrounding the provinces of the Roman Republic is also gradually being lifted. Thus, new dimensions are being added to the traditional picture of the world of the Republic, making it at once more vivid and more convincing.

Nor is it only states, nations, and tribes that have been investigated so painstakingly. Individual families have also been put under the microscope, so to speak. This means, inevitably, well-to-do families who played a part, even if in some instances a minor part, in Roman public life, since it was only they who exercised power and it is only about them that information has survived. Stemmata and marriages (whether attested or inferred), characters and personalities (whether recorded or divined), political activities and associations (whether documented or suspected) have all been subjected, with acumen and pertinacity, to searching examination for any help they may give for unravelling the Roman story. Prosopography has come into its own.

The nineteenth century scholars, needless to say, had not ignored its possibilities, but it has been erudite specialists like Gelzer, Syme, and Badian in the twentieth who have availed themselves of it wholeheartedly, encouraged no doubt by the success which attended Namier's use of the technique for his magisterial studies of eighteenth century England. Some scholars have allowed their exuberant enthusiasm to push the method too far, and legitimate conjecture has sometimes degenerated into unrestrained and ingenious flights of fancy. This has caused Meier and others recently to view it with some disfavour; but, for all that, prosopography has made more penetrating analysis possible and helped to clarify many problems. Above all, it has put an end to the nineteenth century habit of depicting Roman politics in terms of modern party systems.

Prosopography has been particularly helpful for the last century of the Roman Republic and for the first two centuries of the Roman Empire. Amongst other things it has virtually revolutionized interpretations of Augustus. The first of the Roman emperors, or more accurately his charisma, has inevitably been of exceptional interest to a generation familiar with theories of *Führerprinzip*: twentieth century historians, like those of other times, depict their subject in the light of what monopolizes contemporary attention. But prosopography has made a more important and lasting contribution. By laying bare the Italian origins, or at least the Italian connections, of Augustus and his close associates it has revealed that he systematically enlisted non-Roman talents and Italianized the administration of the Empire. This deliberate transformation of the governing caste is a matter of profound consequence for the later history of Rome and indeed of the world.

The Roman Empire has had a huge volume of work devoted to it in our generation, with consequent enrichment of our understanding of it. Once again archaeology together with its by-products, numismatics, papyrology, and above all epigraphy, is largely responsible. In the mid-nineteenth century, the Berlin Academy had encouraged Theodor Mommsen to proceed with his project for a *Corpus Inscriptionum Latinarum*, and by the end of the century a vast amount of material had been collected and published, much of it well calculated to remedy some of the more glaring deficiencies in the literary sources. The majority of the inscriptions belong to the period of the Roman Empire and many of them supply data precisely of the kind needed by the prosopographer. This was realized at once, and scholars went to work with alacrity. In fact the *Prosopographia Imperii Romani* began appearing even before the nineteenth century had reached its end, in 1897 to be precise; and by now continuing epigraphic finds have made a second and enlarged edition of it necessary. By spelling out the careers of men who in many cases are known only from the *Corpus*, the *Prosopographia* has disclosed much about the inner workings and ramifications of the imperial system. And more than the *arcana imperii* have been laid bare. The twentieth century has a much better and surer vision of the immense majesty of the Pax Romana than the scholars of yesteryear with their rather restricted view of the Roman Empire, a view chiefly focussed on the city of Rome and the imperial court. The modern historian's horizon has been widened by the epigraphic material, ransacked and collated by teams of assiduous scholars from many different countries, and it embraces the whole Roman world as never before. The provinces have emerged from their Republican obscurity and the *oikoumene* has displaced Italy as the centre of interest. Appropriately, Mommsen's classic account of *The Provinces of the Roman Empire* is now being superseded by a series of up-to-date studies of the individual provinces.

One period that illustrates better than most this shift of emphasis away from Italy and into the world beyond is the third century A.D. A full, authoritative, trustworthy account of this time of troubles, and especially of the fifty years after the death of Severus Alexander in 235 which came perilously close to witnessing the total disintegration of the Empire, will probably never be written. The literary sources are of the poorest: for much of the period we are dependent, quite literally, on the absurd tissue of inanities, falsehoods, and innuendoes included in the biographies collectively known as the *Historia Augusta*. Nor is there much in the way of documentary material to make good the literary deficiencies: amid the chaos of those tumultuous days there was little time and even less opportunity for the carving of inscriptions. Nevertheless an improved account of the third century has now become possible. The ancillary disciplines, and not least numismatics and papyrology, have contributed something; and it is no longer necessary to parade a mere paraphrase of the Augustan History's ludicrous lives of the emperors with their blatant absurdities as if they were sober history. Today's version provides graphic and authentic details of the local aristocracies and their relations with the central administration as well as of the prevailing anarchy.

Diocletian's restoration of some sort of law and order after 284 has bequeathed source materials that are improved both as to quantity and quality; and the age that shortly afterwards witnessed the triumph of Christianity has always been one of the most intensively studied eras of Roman history. And it still is: the twentieth century has seen no cessation, or slowing down, in the spate of articles and books dealing with the times of Constantine, his rise to power, and his support of the Christian Church. Such studies, however, even though they differ from earlier ones in many details, are for the most part of the type with which the nineteenth century familiarized us, whereas continuing and extensive research has greatly altered other aspects of the Late Empire in recent years.

Today there is a general realization of the radical change that had come over the Roman world by 300 A.D. By then nothing less than a military revolution had taken place, with men under arms constituting a much larger proportion of the population than in the halcyon days of the second century Antonine emperors and with soldiers occupying every post of importance. Furthermore, these military men who ran the Empire and held all its positions of power were not Italians, much less Romans. In other words, the Empire had ceased to be Roman except in name; and the task of the modern student of the "Decline and Fall" is not so much to readdress himself to the by now largely exhausted and somewhat sterile task of chronicling the barbarian invasions as to unravel the process whereby what was truly and genuinely Roman came to be replaced by something very alien. The end of Roman history, like its beginning, has acquired a quite different aspect since the early years of the present century.

The foregoing pages have emphasized how archaeology and the disciplines deriving from it, such as epigraphy, papyrology, and numismatics, contribute to our broadening knowledge and expanding views of Roman history; and it should be added that the art historian also teaches us much, even if our debt to him has gone unrecorded in this paper. But if the student of history has come to depend heavily upon these other disciplines, it is no less true that their exponents, too, cannot avoid invoking the aid of experts in other fields. The archaeologist needs the chemist for radio-carbon datings, the physicist for an estimate of the remanent magnetism in ceramic clay, and the biologist for an assessment of pollens and other vegetable materials; for the epigraphist the skill and advice of the petrologist are frequently necessary; and for the numismatist the metallurgist with his expertise in ores and alloys is uncommonly useful. None of this is very surprising. The study of the Classics by its very nature usually makes those who choose to pursue it interested in all branches of learning and receptive to other subjects.

In recent years the Roman historian has learned much from the social, as well as from the natural sciences. His dependence upon geography was always very close. Nor had he ever been able to ignore political science and economics, despite the absence of an economic framework to most Roman policy. Similarly it is now obvious, and has been for some time, that he cannot remain indifferent to psychology, sociology, and anthropology. Rostovtzeff derived help from all these disciplines for what is universally regarded as one of the most masterly specimens of historical writing in this century, his *Social and Economic History of the Roman Empire* of 1926. But today's Roman historian has progressed far beyond Rostovtzeff and the other pioneers. After taking careful stock of the working methods of the social science disciplines, he wonders whether their field studies, mass surveys, computerization, content analysis, and other techniques cannot be made to serve his purposes too. Just recently there has appeared an *Economy of the Roman Empire* that bears the significant sub-title *Quantitative Studies*; and no particular clairvoyance is needed to foresee that the immediate future is going to find Roman historians engaged more and more on sociological investigations of one sort or another. The century of the common man is bound to devote close attention to *The Man in the Roman Street*, as Harold Mattingly called him in 1947 (without, however, being able to tell us very much about him). Books with titles like *Les Classes sociales dans l'empire romain* and *Social Status and Legal Privilege in the Roman Empire* have already appeared in western countries; and the scholarly world of eastern Europe has naturally been preoccupied for years with studies of this type.

Whether quantification is either practicable or profitable in the case of the data bequeathed from classical antiquity is perhaps doubtful. The surviving material may be too scattered, fragmentary, and casual. But that does not absolve the Roman historian from the duty of seeking to exploit it to the full and in any way he can.

This, in its turn, will involve him in another duty. The interaction of history with the newer social science disciplines suggests that some accommodation ought to be worked out between them, and this is especially true for archaeology. Ideally archaeology should keep in step with documentary history, and so far as Rome is concerned it has usually done so. For other periods and other places, however, intermingling is not always feasible. Archaeologists of the anthropological kind, for instance, often find themselves without any written documents as points of reference, and consequently they tend to become ethnologists. Here there lurks a very real danger. For today's ethnologists seem mainly concerned to enunciate and test theories of social structure. Descriptive archaeology appears to have gone out of fashion, to be replaced by the "new archaeology" that thinks in terms of social stratification. This clearly is another case of studying the past with today's problems chiefly in mind, and it is a somewhat dubious approach. How social structure can be authoritatively studied without reference to political relationships it is not easy to see; and archaeology, unsupported by written records, cannot specify the character of political relationships. The classical archaeologist, therefore, must be on his guard against stumbling into the kind of pitfalls that may have been unintentionally dug by his ethnologist fellow worker, lest his own *a priori* thinking steer his Roman historian colleague in the wrong direction.

Something of the sort may already have happened. In recent years the excavators of the Palatine and other sites in or near Rome have depicted the Iron Age as a period where simple egalitarianism was gradually transformed into a much more complex society closely controlled by a highly centralized power. One cannot help but wonder whether this reconstruction does not owe as much to preconceived notions of social structures as to objective study of the artefacts.

Whether that be the case or not, it is clear that for the historian of Rome there is still a lot that needs doing, and, as there is no reason to think that he will be either hesitant or reluctant to undertake the task, one can confidently expect the next half century to be as exciting and as fruitful for Roman historical studies as the fifty years just ending.

Translating for Liturgy

by J. R. C. Perkin, D. Phil.

The years of our life are three score and ten,
or even by reason of strength fourscore;
Yet their span is but toil and trouble;
they are soon gone, and we fly away.[1]

S uch a jaundiced view was probably justified in the Psalmist's own day, but the quotation is only partially appropriate to Watson Kirkconnell's octogenarian celebrations. "Fourscore," certainly; "toil," indubitably; but "trouble" and the suggestion of a brief and almost unremembered life scarcely fit the impressive achievements and monumental contributions to the humanities made by the former President of Acadia University.

The arbitrary milestones of chronological age really mean very little; our attention should focus on the scholarship rather than the calendar. In which case another verse of Scripture may be cited, for Kirkconnell is part of that select group of whom it may truly be said:

All these won fame in their own generation
and were the pride of their times.[2]

Watson Kirkconnell's life-long passion for Latin, Greek, and Hebrew, first born in honours classics at Queen's and matured during nearly fifty professorial years in the humanities—always as a sympathetic lay neighbour of theological colleges—flowers in his unique contribution to *A Psalter for Everyman*,[3] a diglott translation of the Psalms undertaken in collaboration with Mlle Jeannine Bélanger. Something of the methodology and principles behind that specialized kind of enterprise is glimpsed in the articles by the two translators which appeared in *Meta: Journal des Traductions* in 1970.[4]

Special hazards stand in the way of those who would translate scripture for liturgical use. These hazards arise from the nature of the biblical material, the actual translation of the languages, and the constraints imposed by the liturgical form. Our attention will be confined to translation of New Testament material for congregational use, since this is a newer field of endeavour and has the added challenge that the teaching of Jesus, much of which was probably delivered in Aramaic poetic form, comes to us in Greek prose through which the poetic form is not always clearly discernible.

It is about one hundred years since biblical criticism began to win widespread academic acceptance; it is only about half that time since Gospel criticism underwent a radical change brought about by the work of the Form Critics. They discerned certain common patterns or forms in the gospels, which they viewed not as verbatim reports by reliable eye-witnesses, but as collections of independent units, or *pericopai*, strung together by editors, who provided an appropriate geographical and temporal context for each saying or event. Moreover, they said, the early Christian communities were responsible for the basic forms and may have created some of the content as well. One important element in the Form Critics' work which has been developed during the last fifty years was the recognition that the churches gave rise to the documents rather than *vice versa* and that oral tradition played a significant role in the transmission of the teaching of Jesus.

In the course of time increasingly formative roles were accorded to the churches and parts of the New Testament were identified as catechetical and liturgical. In 1946 G. D. Kilpatrick published a distinctive study, *The Origins of the Gospel according to Saint Matthew*,[5] which examined the sources and circumstances of that gospel. He argues that the decisive influence was liturgical and pointed to Matthew's streamlining of Markan material, his introduction of antitheses and parallelisms, his repetitive use of certain phrases and his feel for rounded and balanced structures.[6] It is not without significance that the familiar (and liturgically common) form of the Lord's Prayer and the Beatitudes is that of Matthew rather than Luke.

In 1952 Philip Carrington published the results of a great deal of research into the nature of Mark's gospel.[7] He advanced the theory that the gospel had been designed and used as a lectionary. Building on the work of the Form Critics he suggested that the basic *pericopai* were given their place and order largely because of factors relating to the structure of the lectionary. His theory can be summed up in the following question and answer: "Is the gospel-unit a liturgical gospel, that is to say, a gospel lection prescribed for a set place in the ecclesiastical order? Nothing forbids us to entertain this hypothesis."[8]

Most major Greek manuscripts have chapter divisions and titles, dating from the fourth century but probably reflecting earlier traditions. The manuscript *B* (Vaticanus) divides Mark into sixty-two chapters, which Carrington believes represent forty-eight units for the Christian year (four units for each of twelve lunar months) and a paschal section of fourteen units, arranged in two groups of seven.[9] Although many details of the theory are open to question it would seem that Carrington has established the distinct possibility that the earliest gospel may have been fashioned around the framework of the church year.

In 1954 Krister Stendahl presented his views on the background out of which Matthew's gospel came. He perceived the influence of catechetical and didactic concerns shaping both the material and its presentation. "The systematizing work, the adaptation towards casuistry instead of broad statements of principles, the reflection on the position of church leaders and their duties, and many other similar features, all point to a milieu of study and instruction."[10]

In the same year F. L. Cross delivered his famous lecture in Oxford in which he theorized that I Peter was a paschal liturgy, used on Easter day at the baptism and first communion of converts.[11]

Although the detail of these theories and several others like them[12] has been challenged, it is clear that contemporary biblical criticism recognizes that the early church did shape the gospel material and that this material was fashioned primarily for public rather than private use.

A word of warning must be immediately registered. Because a scholar thinks, and perhaps even demonstrates, that a particular New Testament passage has a liturgical structure, it does not follow that this structure was imposed or created by the church. It could be that the teaching of Jesus was delivered in a form that contained many poetic features some of which survived the shock of translation from Aramaic into Greek.

In speaking of the teaching of Jesus it is necessary to distinguish between the method and the style he used. Both were typical of his day and cultural context but are so far removed from our experience that a brief comment may be necessary.

One rather surprising result of our emphasis on "resource-material" and "standard references" is that we belong to a generation whose memory, collectively and individually, is short. Rote-learning is frowned upon in schools and our high rate of literacy and the high accessibility of immense resources have decreased the necessity of remembering details. In the first century, when literature was scarce and expensive and where the level of literacy was not high, the only storehouse of information for the average person was his own memory, or the collective memory of his community.

Consequently a major aspect of education—in the case of the Palestinian Jews this was based on the synagogue—was the rote-learning of scriptural passages which had the threefold effect of continuing a reliable oral tradition of the biblical text, training the mind of the student to be receptive and retentive, and developing a feel for those forms which could be readily memorized.

In dealing with older students (perhaps "disciples" would be a preferable English term although such a distinction could not be made in Koine Greek) the Rabbis often used another method which is relevant to a study of the gospels. The Rabbi would introduce a topic and there would be a full discussion of it based on the Law, traditional interpretations of it, personal experiences, and disciples' questions and comments. At the end the Rabbi would provide a poetic summary which would serve as a general reminder of the discussion and also give an indication of the main issue at stake. Disciples were expected to commit these summary statements to memory.

For example, a discussion might take place on the nature of mercy. The various places in the Hebrew Scriptures where the word *hesedh* was found would be examined and the exercise of the quality of mercy would be considered in the light of the disciples' ideas and experience. After the discussion, which could last anything from a few minutes to many hours, the teacher might offer the following summary:

How blest are those who show mercy,
mercy shall be shown to them.[13]

Of course, this does not summarize the whole discussion; what it does is to recall the issue and direct attention to an important factor, namely that "active pity" has a way of spreading and sweetening life.[14] Against this background we see that much of the teaching of Jesus as we have it is not an exhaustive, balanced

91

treatment of any topic, but rather a collection of "texts" to serve his disciples as reminders and pointers.

If we turn to a consideration of the style of Jesus' teaching, the term that immediately commends itself is "poetic," but, appropriate as the word is, we need to be aware of the several meanings it may carry.

The most obvious implication is that some of the teaching of Jesus was cast in the form characteristic of much Hebrew poetry, in which the fundamental feature is a parallelism of ideas. Sometimes the parallelism is synonymous, i.e. a single idea is expressed in two different ways:

> The earth is the Lord's and all that is in it,
> The world and those who dwell therein.[15]

or:

> O Lord, Thou are enthroned for ever,
> Thy throne endures from one generation to another.[16]

At other times the parallelism is antithetic, i.e. a single idea is looked at from two different standpoints, enabling the poet to make a positive and a negative statement. For example:

> The Lord watches over the way of the righteous,
> but the way of the wicked is doomed.[17]

or, in slightly extended form:

> Israel and Judah are not left widowed
> by their God, the Lord of Hosts;
> But the land of the Chaldaeans is full of guilt,
> condemned by the Holy one of Israel.[18]

There are many variations, some quite complicated, on these two basic forms, but an appreciation of the rudiments of Hebrew poetry gives new insights for reading the Old Testament, especially the Psalter, the prophets, and the Wisdom Literature.

Jesus used these poetic forms to the full. Although the translations set out these passages as parts of prose sentences, the original parallel form is clear:

> He makes his sun rise on good and bad alike,
> and sends the rain on the honest and the dishonest.[19]

> Every good tree produces good fruit,
> but the bad tree produces evil fruit.[20]

The alert student of the teaching of Jesus will always be on the lookout for this kind of pattern, either in the Greek as it stands, or in a possible Aramaic form lying behind the Greek.[21]

When we say that the teaching of Jesus is poetic in form we mean something more than that it is characterized by a parallelism of ideas. Eugene Nida and Charles Taber describe poetic language as evidencing multilevel parallelism in " . . . sound, . . . in morphological and syntactic patterns, . . . in lexical choices and especially, perhaps, . . . in semantic structures."[22] It is this, at least as much as the parallelism of idea, which makes the saying memorable. If Winston Churchill had observed: "I doubt whether, in the whole history of warfare, such a small group has ever placed so many people in its debt," it is unlikely that the statement would have attracted any special attention. But put in the form "Never in the field of human conflict has so much been owed by so many to so few," it becomes memorable. We notice that it exemplifies all the requirements of poetic language as specified by Nida and Taber.

Similarly, we notice, Jesus did not say "No one can really have two masters, for he will find himself torn between conflicting claims on his loyalty." He said:

No one can serve two masters;
for either he will hate the one and love the other,
or he will be devoted to the one and despise the other.[23]

There is, however, a third meaning of the term "poetic" as applied to the teaching of Jesus and here we confront one of the most difficult aspects of translation. Stemming from a distinction made by Aristotle, two literary types are commonplace categories in modern criticism—"rhetorical" and "poetic." A useful analysis of these categories and their relevance to biblical scholarship is found in William Beardslee's *Literary Criticism of the New Testament.*[24] He states: "While in terms of 'rhetorical' analysis one can separate the idea from the presentation, in 'poetic' analysis the work makes its impact and finds its meaning by the reader's participation in the form itself."[25]

The two terms usually designate kinds of criticism or analysis, but they have an equal usefulness if applied to the nature of literature itself. In "rhetorical" literature, the intellectual content can be separated from the form in which it is expressed; in "poetic" literature, form is an aspect of content and thus inseparable. In passing one may note that the former kind is comparatively easy to translate; the latter bristles with technical and emotional difficulties.

In this sense the teaching of Jesus is poetic and the translator is challenged to produce a vernacular version which invites the reader or hearer to participate in the form, just as the original did. Although it is the teaching in the gospels which is most obviously "poetic" in Beardslee's sense of the word, many other parts of the New Testament fall into the same category, as we shall see later.

Those who seek to translate for liturgy today are working within a developing tradition of scholarship which makes their task at once easier and more challenging. Easier, because the role played by the early Christian communities in fashioning scripture for their worship and instruction is now recognized; and because the poetic element in the teaching of Jesus is increasingly perceived. More challenging, because it is clearly understood that form and content are not always separate, especially in the gospels, and because unless the translated form is equally inviting as the original the translator need not have laboured at all.

With these thoughts in mind we turn to some consideration of the actual technique of translating New Testament Greek into the English of today.

Familiar as may seem the idea that the art of communication is to enable the recipient to become involved in whatever the communicator has to impart, this whole concept is a modern one. Certainly there were many in ancient times who were skilled communicators and who involved their audiences, but it has been left to this era of mass media and electronic communication to study and analyze the methods these ancients used.

In the realm of translating, there has been a marked shift in emphasis during the present century. Nowhere has this been more clearly stated than in the work by Nida and Taber quoted above. They observe:

> The older focus in translating was the form of the message, and translators took particular delight in being able to reproduce stylistic specialties. . . . The new focus, however, has shifted from the form of the message to the response of the receptor.[26]

A study of the guidelines laid down for the translators of the King James Version indicates that, while theirs was no slavish word-for-word approach, their main concern was to provide an English equivalent for Hebrew and Greek texts—the question of the impact of the English on the reader was not seriously considered. Indeed, one may suppose that the divines reckoned any impact to be more the work of the Holy Spirit than a result of the translator's art.

The King James Version was not a completely new translation; the Bishops' Bible of 1568 was used as a basis and because of the interdependence of earlier translations this meant that the 1611 version was heavily indebted to Tyndale's 1526 New Testament and Coverdale's 1535 complete bible.

The third rule in the translators' guidelines stipulated that ancient ecclesiastical terms like "church" were not to be altered (this looks like an anti-Puritan provision); the fourth is along the same lines and indicates that when a choice of several meanings for one original word is available, the scholars should select the one "which hath been mostly commonly used by the most of the ancient fathers, being agreeable to the propriety of the place and the analogy of the faith."[27]

Nothing should be said to limit the greatness of the achievement of King James's men. They showed phenomenal industry, prodigious scholarship, and a clear sense of what they sought to do. In the preface to their work they criticize both the Puritans and the Papists, the former for wanting to change all the traditional words (and use "washing" instead of "baptism," "congregation" instead of "church," etc.) and the latter for the obscurity of words like "holocausts," "prepuce," and "pascha." Such language, says the preface, may translate the Bible but keep it from being understood. "But we desire that the Scripture may speak like itself, as in the language of Canaan, that it may be understood even of the very vulgar."[28]

Curiously enough, the next major English version was prepared with more rigid guidelines than was the King James Version. In 1870 it was decided to revise the 1611 translation but "to introduce as few alterations as possible into the text of the Authorized Version consistently with faithfulness."[29] In addition to remaining in voluntary bondage to the English of the seventeenth century (in some respects it was that of the sixteenth), the divines who prepared the Revised Version adopted a policy of "one word in the original equals one word in English." The result was a literal and somewhat wooden rendering which never achieved any widespread acceptance, except perhaps in theological colleges, where this very feature made it a useful "crib" for those learning biblical languages!

The comment by Nida and Taber is exemplified in C. H.

Dodd's *Introduction* to the New English Bible New Testament.[30] In outlining the principles used by the New Testament panel of translators Dodd says: "Fidelity in translation was not to mean keeping the general framework of the original intact while replacing Greek words by English words more or less equivalent. . . . We have conceived our task to be that of understanding the original as precisely as we could (using all available aids), and then saying again in our own native idiom what we believed the author to be saying in his."

When translation of the "poetic" type of literature is undertaken—whether its form be that of the poem, the hymn, or the gospel makes little difference—one major requirement is that the translated form should evoke a similar emotion to that produced by the original. Mere substitution of words cannot achieve this. Watson Kirkconnell had some pointed observations along these lines in the introduction to his *European Elegies*[31] ". . . a literal translation is inherently criminal and . . . any verse rendering which sacrifices beauty to philology is a blasphemous offence in its very existence." He goes on to state that a literal translation may describe an experience, but it cannot transmit the actual feeling of that experience. His summary is worth repeating in full:

> In such translation, the translator must cope with a complex incantation of verbal cadences in another language; he must consider the meaning and the imaginative significance of the original; and above all he must seek to communicate the power of emotional experience.[32]

A translator of biblical material whose fame was justly established in 1947 by the publication of *Letters to Young Churches* can be cited as final evidence of the modern understanding of translation. J. B. Phillips lists three tests of a good translation. First, it must not sound like a translation; second, the translator minimizes the intrusion of his own personality; third, he seeks " . . . to produce in the hearts and minds of his readers an effect equivalent to that produced by the author upon his original readers."[33]

The translator of the New Testament into English in this generation has to understand something of the findings of contemporary scholarship as regards the forms of the material on which he works; he must contrive to have one foot in the first century and one in the twentieth; he must also have a religious experience of his own, because the New Testament is written from a context of conviction and commitment and if a translator eliminates that element, or fails to make it clear in up-to-date language, then something vital has been lost.

Such are the constraints of "ordinary" translation; we shall now discuss the extra constraints and possibilities presented by translating for liturgy.

By "translating for liturgy" in the context of New Testament scholarship, we mean rendering the Greek text into English in such a way as to make it suitable for public congregational or antiphonal use.

In many churches, particularly in the non-episcopal communions in North America, there is a tradition of "verse-about" readings from the Psalter. While not denying that such reading can be used to enrich worship, one may note four distinct limitations. First, the parallel forms of Hebrew poetry seldom follow the verse divisions, so the natural poetic flow of a psalm is interrupted rather than demonstrated by this kind of use. Second, the arrangement of the Psalter thus used is usually one pointed for chanting, and never intended to be read. Third, the version is usually that of Coverdale or the King James, and hence full of expressions whose meaning is not immediately apparent to the congregation. Finally, the Psalter, for all its spiritual excellence, is not a distinctively Christian collection. True, a small number of New Testament poems are also found in some liturgies, passages such as the *Magnificat*[34] or the *Nunc Dimittis*,[35] but these are rarely used in the "free" churches and in any case do not exhaust the possibilities of the New Testament as regards poetic sections.

Translating for liturgy does not mean translating a passage into English prose and then arranging the prose into a special form; it means *in one action* rendering the Greek into the form for congregational use, which form, wherever possible, should reflect that of the original.

The difficulty in achieving this lies in the fact that three rather different sets of criteria operate simultaneously and in an interrelated manner. Translation for liturgy must be translation in the sense we have described earlier. There can be no excusing of deliberate alteration of meaning and no justification of changing the sense because the congregation finds the altered form easier to say.

Then there are the liturgical criteria. A congregation should not be asked regularly to repeat passages whose content is peripheral to the central themes of Christianity. Nor should they have to repeat sections whose content is firmly and exclusively rooted in a first century situation. The liturgist seeks to provide material which is central and relevant.

Equally important are those criteria imposed by the congregation itself, composed of many different ages, levels of education and experience, and theological outlooks. A line which needs a very deep breath to say, and an extensive grasp of the English language to understand, has no place in the liturgical form.

In seeking to elaborate the recognition of these three kinds of criteria we shall specify six requirements of the liturgical form with some appropriate examples.

In the first place due weight must be given to the physical appearance of the translated form—its actual lay-out on the page. No academic sophistication must be allowed to blind us to the fact that this generation perceives much more quickly by the eye than by the ear. Although a newspaper is designed as literature, it is eye-catching literature, because the roving eye needs to be arrested before reading can begin.[36]

If a passage of scripture is translated for liturgy, it should have that arresting quality. Lines should be short and yet make, wherever possible, individual sense to the reader. It may be hard for the average clergyman or minister to acknowledge that members of his congregation are not all fully concentrating on worship all the time, but this is the case. Their minds wander and they do not often spend the time before the service silently rehearsing what they will be saying aloud later. Any unfamiliar liturgy, and for some even a familiar one, benefits from having a specific and clear design.

We may illustrate from a passage whose balanced structure is apparent; even in a literal translation the poetic form cannot be totally destroyed. Yet the "liturgical" lay-out rather than the prose form makes its own impact. Compare:

> Now there are varieties of gifts, but the same Spirit; and there are varieties of service, but the same Lord; and there are varieties of working, but it is the same God who inspires them all in every one.[37]

with:

> Now there are different kinds of spiritual gifts,
> But the Spirit is the same;
>
> And there are different kinds of practical service,
> But the Lord is the same;

And there are different kinds of activity,
But it is the same God who is at work
In all of them,
Among all men.[38]

If a group of individuals were given the two forms to read aloud at sight they would surely read the second in a more uniform manner than they would the first.

The second requirement stems immediately from the first. The liturgical form will be laconic rather than polysyllabic. James Montgomery could get away with a line like "with illimitable sway" in a hymn,[39] but a congregation could not *read* that line in unison, although they could and do sing it. Listening to a congregation saying the General Thanksgiving at the point where they say "Thine inestimable love" is enlightening; one doubts whether the uninitiated would have any idea what the phrase was! One also wonders how many people know what "inestimable" means; this leads us into our next point.

Translation for liturgy has to be into simple language. It is not intended for use solely by the devout, or the scholarly, but is also the medium whereby children and those who cannot formulate their own prayers or affirmations are enabled to say something worthwhile and having meaning for them.

In John's gospel we find the word *parakletos* in the Farewell Discourses.[40] It is a great challenge to the exegete who can expatiate at length on the etymology and theology. The translator has to choose one word or phrase and the choices are instructive. The King James Version translates "Comforter," while the Revised Standard Version has "Counselor"; Phillips renders "someone else to stand by you" and the New English Bible has "Advocate."

After trying to assess the relative merits of the different words I concluded that, for liturgical purposes, the word "Helper" was the best choice. "Comforter" is too weak; "Counsellor" too restrictive; Phillips' phrase is too long and the word "Advocate" is rather technical. "Helper" has the merit of being simple, common, and active.[41]

In the fourth instance the liturgical form must be natural. The obvious way to read a passage should be the correct way. A congregational section is often best introduced by an insignificant word, rather than a vital one, as this gives the people time to achieve complete unity by the time they reach the heart of the line. Fortunately both Koine Greek and Hebrew are full of conjunctive particles and the translator only needs to leave these in his rendering at the beginning of the line.

Conversely the last statement of a congregational liturgy should be strong and, if possible, memorable. Thus a rendering of I Corinthians 1:18 would seek to preserve the obvious parallelism of the Greek but instead of the Greek *a b a b* pattern the English has a more natural strength in an *a b b a* arrangement, as follows:

This talk of the cross is nonsense
To those on the road to ruin;
But to us on the road to salvation
It is the power of God.

In Galatians 5:22 there is a list of virtues characteristic of the Spirit and the list ends with a comment translated in the New English Bible as "There is no law dealing with such things as these." As a strong ending to the list of virtues one might prefer

Against such things
There is no law.

Another requirement of the liturgical translation is that it shall have dignity. Not a dignity greater than that of the original (as is sometimes the case with the King James Version), but a dignity which renders it suitable for public corporate use. A striking and somewhat amusing example is provided by a comparative study of three versions of Romans 9:21.

Hath not the potter power over the clay, of the same lump to make one vessel unto honour and another unto dishonour? (KJV)

Surely the potter can do what he likes with the clay. Is he not free to make out of the same lump two vessels, one to be treasured, the other for common use? (NEB)

The potter, for instance, is always assumed to have complete control over the clay, making with one part of the lump a lovely vase, and with another a pipe for sewage. (Phillips)

Admittedly one would hardly call the passage poetic, but the translations make an interesting study from which the middle one emerges as nearer to the language of liturgy than the others which are too obscure and too colloquial respectively.

Similarly, even if one wished to arrange I Corinthians 5:9 into a liturgical pattern it is unlikely that the New English Bible rendering would be thought appropriate: "In my letter I wrote that you must have nothing to do with loose livers"! The King James Version is too old-fashioned: "I wrote to you in an epistle not to company with fornicators," but the Revised Standard Version seems to have caught the right note: "I wrote to you in my letter not to associate with immoral men."

Lastly, translating for liturgy requires, in most cases, a conscious break with the archaic form and an attempt to be modern without being ephemeral or employing the cheap linguistic device. Of course, the decision as to what is ephemeral and what is lasting is not made by the translator, but by the congregations. It is unlikely that the forty-seven men who laboured to produce the King James Version could have predicted the enduring or influential qualities of their work. It is even more unlikely that they could have identified the many idioms and metaphors they were to give to the English language.

Liturgy, especially in such a rapidly-changing world as ours, must somehow preserve the freshness that characterizes so much of the New Testament without fixing itself exclusively in one decade, or even shorter period.

An example may be taken from I Thessalonians 5:14-15. The Revised Standard Version renders:

> And we exhort you, brethren, admonish the idle, encourage the fainthearted, help the weak, be patient with them all. See that none of you repays evil for evil but always seek to do good to one another and to all.

In this quotation the term translated "fainthearted" is *oligopsychous*, literally, "those of little spirit" which strikes me as an acceptable translation and a colourful phrase. My own liturgical version of these verses would be as follows:

> We urge you, brethren,
> To warn the careless;
> Encourage those of little spirit;
> Support the weak;
> Be very patient with all.
> Make sure no one repays wrong with wrong,
> But always pursue good,
> In the fellowship and among all.[42]

There seems to be abundant evidence that Jesus taught in a manner which facilitated the memorization of some of his key statements; evidence also that these statements were transmitted orally long before they were written down and probably long afterwards as well. Parts of other New Testament documents have a poetic structure and were quoted in the writings of the Fathers as well as recited in Christian assemblies.

As a result of the liturgical renewal that has been apparent for some twenty or twenty-five years, many modern congregations are participating comprehensively in worship. To provide worshippers with sections of scripture translated directly into liturgical form is the challenge and opportunity that presents itself to scholars. Such provision not only implants scripture in the minds of the people, it also allows them to experience for themselves some aspects of worship in the early church.

I doubt whether many who translate for liturgy will join Watson Kirkconnell in the ranks of those who

Won fame in their own generation
And were the pride of their times

but they may qualify for general inclusion among those who, in Coverdale's lovely rendering,

found out musical tunes
and recited verses in writing.[43]

Notes

[1] Psalm 90:10 (Revised Standard Version).
[2] Ecclesiasticus 44:7 (New English Bible).
[3] Not yet published.
[4] Kirkconnell, "Translating the Psalter: a Problem of Metre" and Bélanger, "Traduction du Psautier: La Strophique des Psaumes," in *Meta*, Vol. 15, No. 1, March, 1970.
[5] (Oxford: Clarendon Press).
[6] See especially pp. 59-100.
[7] *The Primitive Christian Calendar* (Cambridge: Cambridge University Press, 1952).
[8] Carrington, *op. cit.*, p. 18.
[9] Ibid., p. 26.
[10] *The School of St. Matthew*, quoted from the American edition (Philadelphia: Fortress Press, 1968), p. 29.
[11] *I Peter: A Paschal Liturgy* (London: Mowbray, 1954).
[12] For an example of another kind of approach within the same general area, see Aileen Guilding's study, *The Fourth Gospel and Jewish Worship* (Oxford: Clarendon Press, 1960).

[13] Matthew 5:7.
[14] See H. Daniel-Rops, *Daily Life in the Time of Jesus* (New York: Hawthorn Books Inc., 1962), pp. 112ff. On a distinctive Rabbinic teaching method, see D. Daube, *Journal of Theological Studies*, n.s. Vol. 2 (1951), pp. 45-48.
[15] Psalm 24:1.
[16] Lamentations 5:19.
[17] Psalm 1:6.
[18] Jeremiah 51:5
[19] Matthew 5:45.
[20] Matthew 7:17.
[21] The definitive study in this field is probably still C. F. Burney, *The Poetry of our Lord* (Oxford: Clarendon Press, 1925).
[22] *The Theory and Practice of Translation* (Leiden: Brill, 1969), p. 132.
[23] Matthew 6:24.
[24] (Philadelphia: Fortress Press, 1970).
[25] Beardslee, *op. cit.*, p. 4.
[26] Nida and Taber, *op. cit.* p. 1. See also Geddes MacGregor, *A Literary History of the Bible* (Nashville: Abingdon Press, 1968), pp. 373ff, "Is Translation Possible?"
[27] Quoted in David Daiches, *The King James Version of the English Bible* (Garden City, N.Y.: Anchor Books, 1968 [1941]), p. 169. See also F. F. Bruce, *The English Bible* (London: Lutterworth Press, 1961), Chapter Eight.
[28] Quoted in Bruce, *op. cit.* p. 105.
[29] Ibid., p. 137.
[30] First published in 1961.
[31] (Ottawa: The Graphic Publishers, 1928).
[32] Ibid., p. 23. The relation between the translator's imagination and the inspiration of the original is put in a delightful way in *Poems from XV Languages* (Iowa City: The Stone Wall Press, 1964), p. 3: "Long ago, translation meant direct removal to heaven without an intervening death. This seldom happens to a poem, which too often dies in the act of being translated. . . . To give a suggestion of the text as the poet himself created it, the translator must use his own imagination, always with regard for the true sense."
[33] The quotation may be found in *The New Testament in Four Versions* (London: Collins, 1967), p. xviii.
[34] Luke 1:47-55.
[35] Luke 2:29-32.
[36] There is an interesting discussion of this in the Introduction to R. H. L. Williams' *Prayers for Today's Church* (London: CPAS Publications, 1972).
[37] I Corinthians 12:4-6 (RSV).
[38] This arrangement is cited from my liturgical translation in *The Hymnal* (Baptist Federation of Canada, 1973), No. 674.
[39] In "Hark, the Song of Jubilee," written in the middle of the nineteenth century.
[40] For example, in John 14:16.
[41] It is preferred by Moffatt and Today's English Version, as well as by several German translators.
[42] See *The Hymnal*, No. 677.
[43] Ecclesiasticus 44:5.

Selective Bibliography of Dr. Watson Kirkconnell's Works

covering a period of more than half a century,

compiled by H. W. Ganong, University Librarian, Acadia University

In compiling the following bibliography, use was freely made of two earlier bibliographies published in the *Acadia Bulletin*, one in January 1961 and the other in January 1962. Also, the compiler had access to a list made up by Dr. Kirkconnell for his own personal use, consisting chiefly of material published before 1951. The bibliography appended to Dr. Kirkconnell's memoirs, *A Slice of Canada*, also proved invaluable.

Considerable thought was given to the arrangement of the bibliography, which was finally divided into ten categories, beginning with "Books, pamphlets, and offprints." Within each category, the arrangement is chronological by year, but alphabetical *within* the year. This, it was felt, would enable the reader to follow the development of the author's interests and style, while at the same time it would make it relatively easy for him to locate a specific item, especially if an approximate date were known.

Limitations of space made it impractical to include every published item of which the compiler had knowledge. But while it was realized that any item published by a scholar of Dr. Kirkconnell's stature must be significant to the researcher, it was felt that all material essential to an understanding of the variety and scope of his output had been included.

The bibliography has been divided into ten categories, as follows:

1. Books, pamphlets, and offprints

2. Books, pamphlets, and offprints translated and/or edited by Watson Kirkconnell
3. Serials edited by Watson Kirkconnell
4. Works in collaboration
5. Contributions to collective works
6. Prefaces, forewords, citations
7. Book reviews by Watson Kirkconnell
8. Articles, including poems and translations, published in serials
9. Works completed but unpublished, 1974
10. Articles about Watson Kirkconnell.

(1) Books, pamphlets, and offprints

Kapuskasing, an historical sketch. Kingston, Ontario, 1921.
Victoria county centennial history. Lindsay, Ontario, 1921. Also 2d ed. rev. and updated with the assistance of Frankie L. MacArthur. Lindsay, 1967.
International aspects of unemployment. London, New York, 1923.
Botanical survey of South Victoria. Lindsay, 1926.
"Epilogue to 'Dramatis Personae'." Offprint from *Modern Language Notes*, April 1926. Also reprinted in, Drew, P., ed. *Robert Browning, a collection of critical essays.* 1966.
"Linguistic Laconicism." Offprint from *American Journal of Philology*, January 1927.
"The Bunyan tercentenary." Offprint from *Dalhousie Review*, July 1928.
Canada to Iceland. Lindsay, 1930.
The European heritage: a synopsis of European cultural achievement. London and New York, 1930.
"The genius of Slavonic poetry." Offprint from *Dalhousie Review*, January 1930.
The tide of life and other poems. Ottawa, 1930.
"Petöfi Jelentösége az Uj-Világ Szempontjából," being an inaugural address (in absentia) as honorary member of the Petöfi Society, Budapest, Hungary. Offprint from the Proceedings of the Petöfi Society (*Koszorú, A Petöfi Társaság Közlönye*), November 1932.
The eternal quest. Winnipeg, 1934.
"Icelandic-Canadian poetry." Offprint from *Dalhousie Review*, October 1934.
"Ukrainian poetry in Canada." Offprint from *Slavonic and East European Review*, July 1934.
A Canadian headmaster: a brief biography of Thomas Allison Kirkconnell, 1862-1934. Toronto, 1935.
To Horace (verse). Winnipeg, 1935.
"Canada's leading poet, Stephan G. Stephansson, 1853-1927." Offprint from *University of Toronto Quarterly*, January 1936.

"Hungary's linguistic isolation." Offprint from *Hungarian Quarterly*, January 1936.
"New Canadian letters" (Annual survey, critique and bibliography, 1935 to 1965). Offprints from *University of Toronto Quarterly*, 1937-1966.
"Poetry of Ady." Offprint from *Hungarian Quarterly*, Autumn 1937.
"The new Roman Empire." Offprint from *Dalhousie Review*, April 1937.
"The Rhaetoromanic tradition." Offprint from *Royal Society of Canada. Transactions*, 1937.
"Quintessence of Hungary." Offprint from *Hungarian Quarterly*, Autumn 1938.
Canada, Europe, and Hitler. Toronto, 1939.
"A Skald in Canada." Offprint from *Royal Society of Canada. Transactions*, 1939.
Titus the toad. Toronto, 1939.
"European-Canadians in their press." Offprint from *Canadian Historical Association. Proceedings*, 1940.
European elements in Canadian life. Toronto, 1940.
The flying bull and other tales (verse). Toronto, 1940.
  Also Toronto (© 1949).
  Also Toronto, 1956 (© 1949) (Canadian Classics).
  Also Toronto, 1964 (A Clarke, Irwin Canadian paperback).
The Ukrainian Canadians and the war. Toronto, 1940. Also a Ukrainian version, tr. by Honoré Ewach. (Oxford pamphlets on world affairs, no. C3.)
A Western idyll. Hamilton, 1940.
Canadians all; a primer of national unity. Ottawa, 1941.
Twilight of liberty. Toronto, 1941.
The crow and the nighthawk. Hamilton, 1943. Also published in W. F. Langford. *Realms of Gold*. Toronto, 1958.
Our communists and the new Canadians. Toronto, 1943.
Our Ukrainian loyalists. Winnipeg, 1943.
Canada and immigration. Toronto, 1944.
Seven pillars of freedom. Toronto, 1944. Also 2d (rev.) ed. Toronto, 1952.
"Education in Canada." Offprint from *Culture*, December 1945.
Towards a Christian social order. Toronto, 1945.
"The future of European freedom." Offprint from *Ukrainian Quarterly*, v. 2, no. 3, 1946.
National minorities in the U.S.S.R. Winnipeg, 1946.
The red foe of faith. Toronto, 1946.
"Some Latin analogues of Milton." Offprint from *Royal Society of Canada. Transactions*, 1946.
The Ukrainian agony. Winnipeg, 1946.
"Avitus' epic on the fall." Offprint from *Laval Théologique et Philosophique*, vol. 3, no. 2, 1947.
"Greek history in Greek vocabulary." Offprint from *Royal Society of Canada. Transactions*, 1947.

107

"Canadian communists and the Comintern." Offprint from *Royal Society of Canada. Transactions*, 1948.

The crisis in education. Toronto, 1948.

"The dykes of civilization, inaugural address delivered by Dr. Watson Kirkconnell on the occasion of his installation as president of Acadia University, October 22, 1948." Also printed in the *Acadia Bulletin*, November 1948.

Icelandic history in Icelandic vocabulary. Winnipeg, 1948.

Liberal education in the Canadian democracy. Hamilton, 1948.

A tale of seven cities. Hamilton, 1948.

"Six seventeenth century forerunners of Milton's 'Samson Agonistes'." Offprint from *Royal Society of Canada. Transactions*, 1949.

"Some aspects of Soviet legislation." Offprint from *Royal Society of Canada. Transactions*, 1950.

"Policy post-mortem." Offprint from *Public Affairs*, Autumn 1951.

Stalin's red empire. Winnipeg, 1951. Winnipeg *Free Press* pamphlet no. 38. Reprinted from the editorial pages of the *Free Press*, August-September 1951.

The celestial cycle; the theme of "Paradise Lost" in world literature with translations of the major analogues. Toronto, 1952.

Common English loan words in East European languages. Winnipeg, 1952.

Canada's language policy in education. Paris, 1953. Unesco data-paper for international seminar in Ceylon.

The Kirkconnell pedigree. Wolfville, 1953.

"John Murray Gibbon (1875-1952)." Offprint from *Royal Society of Canada. Proceedings*, 1953.

Canadian toponymy and the cultural stratification of Canada. Winnipeg, 1954.

"Einstein's influence on philosophy." (*Einstein Memorial Symposium, Dalhousie University*, 1955.)

The Mod at Grand Pré: a Nova Scotian light opera in two acts. Wolfville, 1955. Also 2d rev. ed. Wolfville. Condensed versions also printed in the *Acadia Bulletin* and in the *Kentville Advertiser* (Apple Blossom edition).

"Skuli Johnson, 1888-1955," Offprint from *Royal Society of Canada. Proceedings*, 1955.

The place of Slavic studies in Canada. Winnipeg, 1958.

The unconquerable hope. Halifax, 1960.

"Homesickness in several minor keys." Offprint from *Royal Society of Canada. Transactions*, 1961.

The primordial church of Horton. Wolfville, 1963.

Sixteen decades of parsonages: a series of dramatic dialogues. Wolfville, 1964.

That invincible Samson: the theme of "Samson Agonistes" in world literature with translations of the major analogues. Toronto, 1964.

Centennial tales and selected poems. Toronto, 1965.

"Ronald Stewart Longley, 1896-1967." Offprint from *Royal Society of Canada. Proceedings,* 1967.

County of Victoria centennial history. 2d ed. rev. and updated with the research assistance of Frankie L. MacArthur. Lindsay, 1967. Written and published . . . in commemoration of the Centennial of Canadian Confederation.

A slice of Canada: memoirs. Published for Acadia University by the University of Toronto Press, Toronto, 1967.

The fifth quarter-century: Acadia University, 1938-1963. Wolfville, 1968.

"Leviathan, behemoth, kraken. Presidential address." Offprint from *Royal Society of Canada. Transactions,* 1968.

"William John Rose, 1885-1968." Offprint from *Royal Society of Canada. Proceedings,* 1968.

Scottish place-names in Canada. Winnipeg, 1970.

The streets of Wolfville, 1650-1970 Kentville, 1970.

"Translating the Psalter: The Problem of Metre." Offprint from *Meta,* University of Montreal, 1970.

"Ukrainian literature in Manitoba." Offprint from *Mosaic,* University of Manitoba, 1970.

A Georgian house on the post road. Kentville, 1971.

Place-names in King's County, Nova Scotia. Wolfville, 1971.

Awake the courteous echo: the themes and prosody of "Comus," "Lycidas," and "Paradise Regained" in world literature with translations of the major analogues. Toronto, 1973.

"A Canadian Meets the Magyars." Offprint from *Canadian-American Review of Hungarian Studies,* Spring-Fall, 1974.

(2) Books, pamphlets, and offprints translated and/or edited by Watson Kirkconnell

European elegies: one hundred poems chosen and translated from European literature in fifty languages (1st ed.). Ottawa, (© 1928).

North American book of Icelandic verse (ed. and tr.). New York, 1930.

The Magyar muse; an anthology of Hungarian poetry, 1400-1932; edited and translated together with specimens from Ostiak and Vogul. Foreword by Mr. Francis Herczeg. Winnipeg, 1933.

Canadian overtones: an anthology of Canadian poetry written originally in Icelandic, Swedish, Norwegian, Hungarian, Italian, Greek, and Ukrainian, and now translated and edited with biographical, historical, critical, and bibliographical notes. Winnipeg, 1935.

"A Polish miscellany." Offprint from *Slavonic and East European Review,* July 1935.

A golden treasury of Polish lyrics selected and rendered into English, with a foreword by Roman Dyboski (1st ed.). Winnipeg, 1936.

"Ady, Endre. Selected verse: Kinsman of death; Alone with the sea; White lotuses." Offprint from *Slavonic Review,* May 1944.

109

A little treasury of Hungarian verse. Washington, 1947.
The Acadia record, 1838-1953 (4th ed.). Revised and enlarged by Watson Kirkconnell. Wolfville, 1953.
Mickiewicz, Adam. Pan Tadeusz, or The last foray in Lithuania. Translated by Watson Kirkconnell; with an introductory essay by William J. Rose and notes by Harold B. Segel. Toronto, 1962. Also New York, 1968.
Mécs, László. The slaves sing: selected poems, translated by Watson Kirkconnell. DePere, 1964.
Mécs, László. I graft roses on eglantines. Preface by Paul Valéry (Translated by Watson Kirkconnell). Toronto, 1968.
Woodworth, Elihu, 1771-1853. *The diary of Deacon Elihu Woodworth.* Transcribed by Frederick Irving Woodworth, 1962. Edited by Watson Kirkconnell, 1972. Wolfville, 1972.
Rest, perturbèd spirit: the life of Cecil Francis Lloyd, 1884-1938. Windsor, N.S., 1974.

(3) Serials edited by Watson Kirkconnell

The Authors' Bulletin (quarterly). Winnipeg, vols. iii and iv, 1925-1927.
Manitoba Poetry Chapbook. Winnipeg, 1933. In seven languages.
Canadian Poetry Magazine (quarterly). Toronto, vols. viii and ix, 1944-1946.

(4) Works in collaboration

Arany, János. *The death of King Buda:* a Hungarian epic poem by János Arany. Rendered into English by Watson Kirkconnell in collaboration with Lulu Putnik Payerle; with a foreword by Géza Voinovich and notes by Dr. Árpád Berczik. Cleveland, 1936.
(With M. I. Mandryka) *The Ukrainian question.* Winnipeg, 1940.
(With Séraphin Marion) *The Quebec tradition, an anthology of French-Canadian prose and verse.* Selected by Séraphin Marion and translated into English by Watson Kirkconnell. Montreal, 1946.
(With A. S. P. Woodhouse) *The humanities in Canada.* Ottawa, 1947.
Prince Ihor's raid against the Polovtsi. Translated by Paul C. Crath, versified by Watson Kirkconnell. Saskatoon, 1947.
(With E. A. Collins) *Cape Breton.* Words by Watson Kirkconnell. Music by E. A. Collins. Wolfville, 1948 (score).
(With E. A. Collins) *Graduation anthem.* Words by Watson Kirkconnell. Music by E. A. Collins. Wolfville, 1949 (score).
(With E. A. Collins) *Nova Scotia suite for voice and piano.* Words by Watson Kirkconnell, music by E. A. Collins. Wolfville, 1950 (score).
(With E. A. Collins) *The Mod at Grand Pré; opera in two acts* (1956). Libretto: Watson Kirkconnell; music (rev. 1960): E. A. Collins. New York, 1960 (score).

(With C. H. Andrusyshen, ed. and tr.) *The Ukrainian poets, 1189-1962.* Selected and translated into English verse by C. H. Andrusyshen and Watson Kirkconnell. Toronto, 1963.
(With C. H. Andrusyshen) Shevchenko, Taras. *Poetical works.* Translated by C. H. Andrusyshen and Watson Kirkconnell. Toronto, 1964.
(With B. C. Silver) *Wolfville's historic homes.* Wolfville, 1967, 2nd rev. edition, 1974.

(5) Contributions to collective works

Sixteen poems from Swedish, Danish, Icelandic, Norwegian, Polish, and Russian. In *Program of New Canadian Folk Song and Handcraft Festival.* Winnipeg, 1928.
Ten poems. In Manning, C. A., ed. *An anthology of Czechoslovak verse.* New York, 1928.
Three poems. In Cowperthwaite, W. A. and Marshall, E. K., eds. *A treasury of verse for secondary schools.* London, 1929. (Authorized by the Department of Education for use in the secondary schools of Manitoba.)
"Petöfi, 1823-1849." A contribution to *A Petöfi Leleplezési Unnepélyről Emléklapok,* ed. by Király Imre. Cleveland, 1930.
Biographies of Albert Lozeau, J. W. Bengough, John Hughes, W. D. Otter, Jules Tremblay, and Murray Wrong. In *A standard dictionary of Canadian biography,* vol. I, ed. by Charles G. D. Roberts and A. L. Tunnell. Toronto, 1934.
Translations of eight poems (four Hungarian, three Icelandic, one Albanian). In *All nations song book,* edited by the Church of All Nations. Toronto, 1936.
A brochure of twenty-nine verse translations from Magyar. In *Budapest University Chorus program.* New York, 1937.
"Manitoba Symphony." In Lodge, R. C., ed. *Manitoba essays.* Toronto, 1937.
"The literature of the New Canadians." A chapter in The Canadian Broadcasting Corporation. *Canadian literature today.* Toronto, 1938.
"Canada's war effort, 1942, 1943, 1944." Contributed to *Americana Annual.* New York, 1943, 1944, 1945.
"The settlement of Canada." Contributed to the *Book of Knowledge,* 1943.
"Forefathers' Eve, Part III, Act I, scenes 7-9" and "To my Russian friends." In *Mickiewicz ; Adam. Poems.* Translated by various hands and edited by George Rappall Noyes. New York, 1944.
"Canada." Contributed to *Americana Annual.* New York, 1945.
"Manitoba." Contributed to *Grolier Encyclopedia,* 1946.
"The trapper and the bears" (poem). In, Robins, John, ed. *A pocketful of Canada.* Toronto, 1946.
"Ukrainian literature." In *Columbia dictionary of European literature.* New York, 1947.

111

"The road to Bethlehem" (poem). In Morriss, James, ed. *Masterpieces of religious verse.* New York and London, 1948.

"Ukrainians in Canada." In *Encyclopedia Slavonica.* Edited by S. J. Roucek. New York, 1949.

"Education." Being Chapter xix in Brown, George, ed. *Canada.* Berkeley, 1950, The United Nationas Series.

Several poems. In Allward, Martin S., ed. *20th century Scandinavian poetry.* Mullsjö, Sweden, 1951.

"Salandra and Milton." In *Ukrainian Free University Festschrift.* Munich, 1951.

Contributions to Creekmore, Hubert, ed. *A little treasury of world poetry.* New York, 1952.

Contribution to Percival, W. P., and Brush, J. G. S., eds. *Poems to enjoy.* Toronto, 1955.

Some twenty-eight translations. In Kunz, Egon F., ed. *Hungarian poetry.* Sydney, Australia, 1955.

"The humanities." Being chapter 17 in Katz, Joseph, ed. *Canadian education today.* Toronto, 1956.

"Translation of Epilogue to *Pan Tadeusz.*" In Lednicki, Waclaw, ed. *Adam Mickiewicz in world literature, a symposium.* Berkeley, 1956.

"Tapestry of Hungarian literature." In *World literature.* Pittsburgh, 1956.

Two poems. In Gill, J. L., and Newell, L. H., eds. *Invitation to poetry.* London, 1956.

Contribution to Kingston, E. F., ed. *Poems for pleasant study.* Toronto, 1957.

Three translations (Tuwim, Slonimsky, Palagyi). In Ausubel, Nathan, ed. *A treasury of Jewish poetry.* New York, 1958.

Contribution to Simányi, Tibor, ed. *The people of Kossuth.* Vienna, 1959.

"Thoughts on education." In Chalmers, R. C., ed. *Challenge and response.* Toronto, 1960.

"Religion and philosophy: an English-Canadian point of view." A chapter in Wade, Mason, ed. *Canadian dualism: studies of French-English relations.* Toronto, 1960.

Contribution to Humble, A. H., ed. *Lyric and longer poems.* Toronto, 1960.

"A Scotch-Canadian discovers Poland." In Turek, Wiktor, ed. *The Polish past in Canada.* Toronto, 1960.

Twenty-three translations. In McLaughlin, Richard, and Slack, Howard E., eds. *1,000 years of European poetry; music of the mind: an anthology.* New York, 1963.

"The Baptist Federation of Canada." In, *Baptist Advance: the achievements of the Baptists of North America for a century and a half.* Nashville, Tenn., 1964.

"The dynamo king." In McKellar, H. D., ed. *Five score and more; poems for secondary schools.* Agincourt, 1964.

112

Some thirty-one translations. In Gillon, Adam, and Krzyzanowski, Ludwik, eds. *Introduction to modern Polish literature: an anthology of fiction and poetry*. New York, 1964.
Translations from the Icelandic of Hallgrimur Pétursson. In Hallmundson, Halberg, ed. *An anthology of Scandinavian literature from the Viking period to the twentieth century*. New York, 1966.
"Nouvelle-Ecosse." In *Dix Provinces: Un Canada*. Quebec, 1967.
"To Sándor Petöfi" (poem), with Magyar translation by Ferenc Fáy. In *Szabadságharcunk a világirodalomban*. Munich, 1973.
Also additional contributions to: *All Nations Song Book, Book of Knowledge, Collier's Encyclopedia, Commonwealth Universities Yearbook, Encyclopedia Americana, Encyclopedia Britannica, Encyclopedia Canadiana, Grolier Encyclopedia*.

(6) Prefaces, forewords, citations

Kun, Andor. *A country men forget: a little book of 1,000 facts about 1,000 year-old Hungary*.... Authorized English version (with a foreword by Watson Kirkconnell). Winnipeg, 1937.
Nemes, Gusztáv. *Kanada Történelme* (History of Canada) with "Elöszó" (foreword) by Watson Kirkconnell. Winnipeg, 1941.
Tosevic, Dmitri Jovan. *Third year of guerilla* (with a foreword by Watson Kirkconnell). Toronto, 1943.
Szécskay, George. *Öszi Tarlózas Ötven Éves Mezön* (with a foreword by Watson Kirkconnell). Cleveland, 1947.
Ukrainians in Canada; business yearbook, 5th, 1948/49 (with a foreword, "Salute to achievement," by Watson Kirkconnell). Winnipeg, 1948.
Prychodko, Nicholas. *One of the fifteen million* (with a foreword by Watson Kirkconnell). Toronto, 1952.
Pidhainy, D. A. *Islands of death* (preface by Watson Kirkconnell). Toronto, 1953.
Grosz, Joseph, *The black piano* (with a foreword by Watson Kirkconnell). 1956.
Turek, Wiktor. *The Polish past in Canada; contributions to the history of the Poles in Canada and of Polish-Canadian relations* (Introduction by Watson Kirkconnell). Toronto, 1960.
Del Plaine, C. W. *Second growth; the saga of a "new boy in town"* (Foreword by Watson Kirkconnell) (1st ed.). New York, 1961.
Smith, Ernest Chalmers. *Department of biology, Acadia University, 1910-1960* (with a foreword by Watson Kirkconnell). Kentville, 1961.
Mansergh, Nicholas. *South Africa, 1906-1961; the price of magnanimity* (with a foreword by Watson Kirkconnell). New York, 1962 (Harvey T. Reid lectures, 3rd series, 1960. Acadia University).
Robinson, Kenneth. *The dilemmas of trusteeship; aspects of British colo-*

113

nial policy between the wars (with a preface by Watson Kirkconnell). London, 1965.

Preface to the Centennial symposium. *Royal Society of Canada. Transactions*, 1967.

Royal Society of Canada. Presentation of Lorne Pierce Medal to Robert Duer Clayton Finch. Citation by W. Kirkconnell and response of Prof. Finch (In *Royal Society of Canada. Proceedings*, 1968).

Royal Society of Canada. Presentation of Tyrrell medal to G. W. L. Nicholson. Citation by W. Kirkconnell (In *Royal Society of Canada. Proceedings*, 1968).

Rudnyckyj, Jaroslav Bohdan. *Manitoba: mosaic of place names*, compiled by J. B. Rudnyckyj (with an introduction by Watson Kirkconnell). Winnipeg, 1970.

(7) Book reviews by Watson Kirkconnell

Review of Lloyd, C. F. *Landfall, collected poems.* 1935. (In *Dalhousie Review*, 1935.)

Review of Moellman, Albert, *Das Deutschtum in Montreal*, 1937. (In *Canadian Historical Review*, June 1938.)

Review of Lehmann, Heinz. *Das Deutschtum in Westkanada*, 1938. (In *Canadian Historical Review*, September 1939).

Review of Stubbs, Roy St. George. *Lawyers and laymen in Western Canada.* 1939. (In *Manitoba Law Review*, 1939.)

"The cultural record" (a review of Shipley, Joseph T. *Encyclopedia of literature.* 1946. And of Schmidt, Wilhelm. *Rassen und Völker in Vorgeschichte* and *Geschichte des Abendlandes.* 1946) (In *Revue de l'Université d'Ottawa*, janvier 1948, juin 1950 and *University of Toronto Quarterly*, January 1948.)

"The Lithuanian tragedy": a review of Jurgela, Constantine R. *History of the Lithuanian nation.* 1948 (Lithuanian Cultural Institute) (In *Plain Talk*, April 1948.)

Review of Lysenko, Vera. *Men in sheepskin coats, a study in assimilation.* 1947. (In *Opinion*, July 1948.)

Review of Ellis, M. B. *Robert Charbonneau et la création romanesque.* 1948. (In *French Review*, 22 October 1948. Also in *Culture*, January 1948.)

Review of Cerulli, Enrico. *Etiopi in Palestina, storia della Communità Etiopica de Gerusalemme* 1943-47. (In *Revue de l'Université d'Ottawa*, octobre-décembre, 1948.)

Review of Rose, W. J. *Poland old and new.* 1948. (In *Dalhousie Review*, April 1949. Also in *Queen's Quarterly*, Winter 1948/49.)

Review of *Ivan Franko, the poet of the Western Ukraine. Selected poems*, tr. with a biographical introduction by Percival Cundy. 1948. (In *Modern Language Quarterly*, September 1950.)

Review of Aigar, Peteris. *Red Train. 1951.* And of Kangro, Bernard.

Earthbound. 1951. (In *American Slavic and East European Review*, 1951.)

Review of Beck, Richard. *History of Icelandic poets, 1800-1940.* 1950. (In *Scandinavian Studies*, February 1951.)

Review of Mirchuk, Ivan. *Ukraine and its people.* 1949. (In *Revue de l'Université d'Ottawa*, juillet-septembre 1951.)

Review of Beamish, Tufton. *Must night fall?.* 1950. (In *Dalhousie Review*, Autumn 1951.)

Review of Einarsson, Stefan. *History of Icelandic prose writers, 1800-1940.* 1948. (In *Journal of English and Germanic Philology*, July 1949.)

Review of *White Book on Hungarian prisoners of war.* (In *Dalhousie Review*, Spring 1953.)

Review of Walters, Thorstina. *Modern sagas.* 1953. (In *Dalhousie Review*, Winter 1954.)

Reviews of Veyret, Paul. *La population du Canada.* 1953. And of Yuzyk, Paul. *The Ukrainians in Manitoba.* 1953. (In *Canadian Historical Review*, March 1954.)

Review of Kertész, István. *Diplomacy in a whirlpool; Hungary between Nazi Germany and Soviet Russia.* 1953. (In *Dalhousie Review*, Spring 1955.)

Review of Kertész, Fred. *The fate of East Central Europe.* 1956. (In *Dalhousie Review*, Winter 1957.)

Review of *Index translationum: international bibliography of translations.* (In *Unesco Publications Review*, March 1956, February 1959, February 1960.)

Review of Lindal, W. J. *The Saskatchewan Icelanders.* 1955. (In *Dalhousie Review*, Summer 1956.)

Review of *Adam Mickiewicz, 1798-1855.* (*Unesco Publications Committee, Canada, Review* no. 6, January 1957.)

Review of Francis, E. K. *In search of Utopia: the Mennonites in Manitoba.* (In *Canadian Historical Review*, March 1957.)

Review of Franko, Ivan. *Poems and stories*, tr. by John Weir. 1956. (In *Canadian Forum*, March 1957.)

Review of Ivison, Stuart and Rosser, Fred. *The Baptists of Upper and Lower Canada before 1820.* 1957. (In *Queen's Quarterly*, Summer 1957.)

Review of Kertész, Fred. *The fate of East Central Europe.* 1956. (In *Dalhousie Review*, Winter 1957.)

Review of Lesins, Knuts. *The wine of eternity: short stories from the Latvian.* 1957. (In *Dalhousie Review*, Spring 1958.)

Review of Klonowicz, Sebastjan Fabjan. *The boatman*, tr. from the Polish by Marion M. Coleman. 1958. (In *European Journal*, Spring 1959.)

Review of Pierce, Lorne. *A Canadian nation.* 1960. (In *Maritime Baptist*, March 23, 1960.)

Review of Rilke, Rainer Maria. *Letters to a young poet.* Tr. by K. W. Maurer. 1954. (In *Canadian Poetry Magazine*, Winter 1959/60.)

Review of Sissons, C. B. *Church and state in Canadian education.* 1959. (In *Canadian Journal of Theology,* Autumn 1960.)
Review of Lord, Albert B. *The singer of tales.* 1960. (In *Dalhousie Review,* Autumn 1960.)
Review of Slavutych, Yar. *Oasis.* (In *Books Abroad,* Spring 1962.)
Review of Cohen, J. M. *A history of Western literature.* 1961. (In *Queen's Quarterly,* Winter, 1962.)
Review of Duczynska, Ilona and Polyani, Karl, eds. *The plough and the pen.* 1963. (In *Dalhousie Review,* Summer 1963.)
Review of Gillon, Adam. *Selected poems and translations.* 1962. (In *Acadia Bulletin,* January 1963.)
Review of Turek, Wiktor. *The Polish language press in Canada.* 1962. (In *Queen's Quarterly,* Winter 1963.)
Review of Green, Thomas. *The descent from heaven; a study in epic continuity.* 1963. (In *Queen's Quarterly,* Spring, 1965.)
Review of Hatto, Arthur T., ed. *Eos.* (In *Literature East and West,* May 1967.)
"Soviets' hunger for peace," a review of Niemeyer, Gerhart. *A deceitful peace.* 1971. (In *Canada Month,* October 1971.)

(8) Articles, including poems and translations, published in serials

"The flora of Kapuskasing and vicinity." *Canadian Field Naturalist,* May 1919.
"The Amerindian archaeology of Victoria County." *Watchman-Warder,* October 1920.
"The first authentic story of our internment camps." *Maclean's Magazine,* September 1, 1920.
"Fort Henry, 1812-1914." *Queen's Quarterly,* July 1920.
"Bryophyta of Boskung." *Canadian Field Naturalist,* November 1921.
"The Trenton Cuesta." *Canadian Mining Journal,* March 18, 1921.
"Amid nationalist riots in Egypt." *Watchman-Warder,* August 24, 1922.
"Britain's present-day conditions." *Watchman-Warder,* July 13, 1922.
"Factors in French policy." *Watchman-Warder,* July 27, 1922.
"Germany's crisis." *Watchman-Warder,* July 20, 1922.
"Historic ruins and landscapes." *Watchman-Warder,* July 10, 1922.
"The inspiration of Greece." *Watchman-Warder,* August 10, 1922.
"The Ku Klux Klan of Italy." *Watchman-Warder,* August 3, 1922.
"A pilgrimage from Egypt to Jerusalem." *Watchman-Warder,* August 31, 1922.
"The patriarch of Boskung." *Echoes* (Minden, Ont.), July 21, 28, August 4, 11, 1922.
"With Turk and Greek in Asia Minor." *Watchman-Warder,* July 17, 1922.
"Mechanism and meliorism." *Challenge,* September 28, 1925.

"The Ti-Jean stories." *Canadian Forum*, September 1923.
"Translations from Greek poets." *Vox Wesleyana*, December 1924.
"The Greek epigram." *Queen's Quarterly*, January 1925.
"Mendelism and cephalic index." *American Journal of Physical Anthropology*, October 1925.
"A mummified city: the archaeology of Pompeii." *Grain Grower's Guide* (Winnipeg), September 2, 1925.
"The palaeogeography of Ontario." *School*, October 1925.
"The patriarch of Western letters." *Manitoba Free Press*, December 7, 1925.
"Poems from the Danish." *Manitoban*, November 5, 1925.
"Founder of modern Slovak literature." *Manitoban Literary Supplement*, October 28, 1926.
"Frederick Philip Grove." *Canadian Bookman*, April 1926.
"John Maclean." *Canadian Bookman*, September 1926.
"Karel Capek and R. U. R." *Vox Wesleyana*, December 1926.
"Physiology and phonetic change." *Manitoban*, October 7, 1926.
"Research into Canadian rural decay." *Eugenics Review*, July 1926.
"Celtic and Finno-Ugric poetry." *Western Home Monthly*, November 1927.
"Northern Slavic poetry." *Western Home Monthly*, October 1927.
"Poetry of the Balkans." *Western Home Monthly*, June 1927.
"Romance poetry." *Western Home Monthly*, July 1927.
"Scandinavian poetry." *Western Home Monthly*, August 1927.
"South German poetry." *Western Home Monthly*, September 1927.
"Three Greek choruses." *Vox*, December 1927.
"Western immigration." *Canadian Forum*, July 1928.
"A French league plan." *Interdependence*, June 1929.
"Russia's foreign policy." *Western Home Monthly*, May 1929.
"The cultural value of Icelandic." *Jón Bjarnason Academy. Annual*, December 1931.
"A Magyar miscellany." Serially in *Slavonic and East European Review*, 1931, 1938, 1943, 1945.
"Rumanian troops in Budapest." *Winnipeg Free Press*, November 27, 1931.
"The adventurous heart." *National Home Monthly*, November 1932.
"Disarmament." *Journal des Poètes* (Brussels), March 1932.
"Manitoba limericks." Serially in one hundred issues of *Winnipeg Free Press*, November 1932-January 1933.
"The path of Demos." *University of Manitoba Quarterly*, October 1932.
"La poésie française au Canada." *Journal des Poètes* (Brussels), February 27, 1932.
"Prairie summer," "After fever," and "Blood," tr. into Ukrainian verse, by Honoré Ewach. *Ukrayinsky Holos* (Winnipeg), September 21, 1932.
"Towards a national literature." *Authors' Bulletin*, May 1932.

117

"Ta Grammata" (the way of the scholar). *Dalhousie Review*, July 1932.
"Writing on the prairie." *Authors' Bulletin*, September 1932.
"Christmas in Flanders." *National Home Monthly*, December 1933.
"Eight millenia after." *Crucible*, April 1933.
"The land of the north wind." *Lögberg*, August 10, 1933.
"Saskatchewan limericks." Serially in fifty issues of *Regina Leader-Post*, January-March, 1933.
"The way of the healer." *Manitoba Medical Association Journal*, March 1933.
"An academic poet in Magyar America." *Kanadai Magyar Ujság*, May 29, 1934.
"Art in Southern Hungary." *Kanadai Magyar Ujság*, April 20, 1934.
"The first Magyar-American poets." *Kanadai Magyar Ujság*, March 9, 1934.
"The Gradiad." *Vox*, June 1934.
"The lay of Elijah." *Canadian Forum*, August 1934.
"Lilacs and coffee houses." *Winnipeg Free Press*, September 24, 1934.
"Proletarian poetry." *Canadian Spectator*, November 22, 29, 1934.
"Ukrainian Canadiana." *Canadian Forum*, January 1934.
"Ukrainian poetry in Canada." *Slavonic Review*, July 1934.
"The Ayrshire muse." *Canadian Forum*, February 1935.
"Fiction and drama; brief essay on the Ukrainian writings of Dmytro Sollanych and Alexis Luhowy." *Novy Shlyakh*, August 27, 1935.
"Georgius V, Rex et Imperator." *National Home Monthly*, May 1935.
"Hogy lett belölem nyelvész és költö." *Zászlónk*, February 15, 1935.
"Maintaining our educational highways." *Western School Journal*, March 1935.
"Ode on the death of Marshal Joseph Pilsudski." *Evening Tribune* (Winnipeg), May 24, 1935; also in *Warsaw Weekly*, June 14, 1935.
"Progresivi tempes in novial." *Novialiste*, September 1935.
"Scholarship in Szeged." *Kanadai Magyar Ujság*, January 4, 1935.
"Some fundamentals of poetry." *Western School Journal*, December 1935 and January 1936.
"To Ignace Jan Paderewski." *Gazeta Katolicka*, November 6, 1935.
"A Ukrainian expressionist." *Novy Shlyakh*, October 1, 1935.
"Ukrainian poetry." *New Magazine*, October 1935.
"Unesmi impresiones de novial." *Novialiste*, March 1935.
"War and peace in the history class." *Western School Journal*, June 1935.
"Canadian poets." *Music and Arts Magazine*, May 1936.
"Canadian-Polish cultural relations." *Warsaw Weekly*, July 17, 1936.
"The clue of the twisted letter" (murder mystery). *National Home Monthly*, November 1936.
"Hungary's problem of self-defence." *Young Magyar-American*, June 1936.
"Icelandic lyrics." *Lögberg*, May 7, 1936.

"Icelandic poetry today." *Life and Letters Today*, Winter 1936.
"In praise of Budapest." *Young Magyar-American*, March 1936.
"The Kisfaludy Society Centenary." *Young Magyar-American*, May 1936.
"The languages of Britain." *Winnipeg Free Press*, October 15, 1936.
"Leif Erikson." *Norge-Canada*, May 1936.
"A Lilliputian calendar." *Young Magyar-American*, April 1936.
"A Magyar bibliography." *Young Magyar-American*, May 1936.
"A mystery play." *Young Magyar-American*, March 1936.
"Norse names in Scotland." *United Scottish Association. Annual*, October 1936.
"A Parnassian sunset." *Young Magyar-American*, March 1936.
"Pilsudski's heart." *Gazeta Katolicka*, May 1936.
Also in *Warsaw Weekly*, July 17, 1936.
Also in *Czas*, May 1936.
"Poets of Transylvania." *Young Magyar-American*, April 1936.
A Primer of Hungarian. Serially in *Young Magyar-American*, 1936-1939.
"The Sekler folk ballad." *Young Magyar-American*, March 1936.
"Some Ukrainian publications" ("Deyaki Ukrainski Publikatsiyi"). *Kanadiysky Farmer*, June 24, 1936.
"Ukrainska poeziya v Kanadi." *Vistnyk*, June 1936.
"Verse and prose from Szeged." *Young Magyar-American*, March 1936.
"Writers of South Hungary." *Young Magyar-American*, May 1936.
"The passing of Ralph Connor." *Canadian Thinker*, December 1937.
"Poésie canadienne." *Courrier des Poètes* (Brussels). March 15, 1937.
Pushkin, A. S. Some poems translated from the Russian. *Winnipeg Free Press*, February 27 and May 29, 1937.
"Recent Polish poetry." *Life and Letters Today*, Winter 1937.
"Three prairie authors." *Winnipeg Free Press*, November 6, 1937.
"A Ukrainian-Canadian lyrist." *Novy Shlyakh*, March 16, 1937.
"Christmas poetry." *Canadian Thinker*, December 1938.
"Clouds over Czecho-Slovakia." *Vox*, December 1938.
"Doctor's tale of the captain's cat" (poem). *Canadian Poetry Magazine*, June 1938.
"Glimpses from a trip to Hungary." *Young Magyar-American*, December 1938.
"A latter-day Job." *Vox*, June 1938.
"Loan-words in Latin." *Manitoba Arts Review*, Fall 1938.
"The Manitoba Stonehenge." *Winnipeg Free Press*, March 5, 1938.
"Minorities in Europe." *Canadian Thinker*, November 1938.
"The Red River tragedy." *Winnipeg Free Press*, May 1938.
"Subcarpathian Ruthenia." *Evening Tribune* (Winnipeg), December 9, 1938.
"The tale of the abandoned farmhouse." *Winnipeg Free Press*, May 1938.

"Tale of the Angus bull" (poem). *National Home Monthly*, March 1938.
"Travellers in old Budapest." *Young Magyar-American*, December 1938.

Syndicated material. The following articles were written during European travel and syndicated to *Vancouver Province, Calgary Herald, Edmonton Journal, Winnipeg Evening Tribune, Hamilton Spectator,* and *Ottawa Citizen* during August and September, 1938:

"Berlin, strength and malaise"
"A Czecho-Polish sore spot"
"Czecho-Slovakia, a wasp's nest"
"Danzig's policy of strife"
"Eastern Poland fears Moscow"
"Hungary celebrates King Stephen's year"
"Hungary's farm problems"
"The Italian race"
"Italy: Fascism presents the Augustan empire"
"The melancholy Dane"
"Open air drama in summer Europe"
"Religious contrasts in contemporary Hungary"
"Rumania's iron hand"
"Sweden, a civilized nation"
"Vienna, political tragedy and economic hope"
"Warsaw, a modern city"
"Wealth and poverty in the new Rumania"
"Wings over the Baltic states"
"Workmen's housing in Oslo."

The following articles were syndicated in fifteen Manitoba weeklies in October, 1938:

"Jugoslavia today"
"The languages of Canada"
"The White Russians."

"Canada and the refugees." *Western Baptist*, June 1939.
"Canada at war." *Western Baptist*, October 1939.
"Canada to her king." *National Home Monthly*, May 1939.
"The foreign policy of Hungary." *Young Magyar-American*, January 1939.
"The Hellenic tradition." *Ahepa Convention. Annual*, 1939.
"Old Magyar folk-songs," translated from the Magyar. *Young Magyar-American*, February 1939.
"Our foreign language red press." *Evening Tribune* (Winnipeg), November 18, 1939.
"Poland faces war." *Evening Tribune*, August 28, 1939.
"Poland the intrepid." *Evening Tribune*, August 26, 1939.
"Polish stock-taking." *Evening Tribune*, August 27, 1939.

"The price of Christian liberty." *Western Baptist*, October and November, 1939.
"September 1939." *Winnipeg Free Press*, September 16, 1939.
"Ten centuries of Danzig." *Evening Tribune*, August 25, 1939.
"With the Baptists of Budapest." *Western Baptist*, February 1939.

The following articles were syndicated in the *Evening Citizen* (Ottawa), *Evening Tribune* (Winnipeg) and *Edmonton Journal* in October and November 1939:

"Canada's Magyars and Finns"
"Canada's Russians, Czechs and Croats"
"The Canadian Germans"
"The Canadian Italians"
"The Canadian Jews"
"The Canadian Poles"
"The Canadian Scandinavians"
"The Canadian Ukrainians."

"Canada and European peace." *Country Guide*, February 1940.
"Canadians all." *Newtonian*, 1940.
"A new year in wartime." *Western Baptist*, January 1940.
"The Scandinavian tradition." *Lögberg*, February 1940.
"The trapper and the bears" (poem). *Saturday Night*, November 16, 1940.
"War aims and Canadian unity." *Evening Tribune*, January 27, 29, 1940.

The following article was syndicated in *Evening Tribune, Edmonton Journal*, and *Hamilton Spectator* in June, 1940:

"Acid test for saboteurs."

"Canadian amalgam." *Common Ground*, Autumn 1941.
"Canadian tribute to Paul Teleki." *Saturday Night*, April 12, 1941.
"Democracy for Canadians." *Canadian School Journal*, June 1941.
"Easter" (poem). *National Home Monthly*, April 1941.
"New-Canadian poetry." *Canadian Poetry Magazine*, August 1941.
"Race and nationality in Canada." *Native Son*, April 1941.
"Aesop for Canadians." *Evening Telegram*, August 4, 1942.
"Author looks at the library." *Ontario Library Review*, May 1942.
"Leftist Ukrainian halls." *Saturday Night*, December 5, 1942.
"Meeting new Canadians." *World Friends*, July 1942.
"Our communist revolutionaries are not Russian." *Saturday Night*, December 12, 1942.
"Poetry and national life." *Canadian Poetry Magazine*, October 1942.
"Polish literature." *Poles in Canada*, 1942.
"A salute." *Icelandic Canadian*, December 1942.

"The twilight of Canadian Protestantism." *Canadian Baptist*, December 1, 1942.

"We're all Canadians." *Toronto Star Weekly*, May 2, 1942.

"A worthy enterprise." *Canadian Ukrainian Review*, February 1942.

"The world I want to see after the war." *Quest*, October 11, 1942.

"The agony of Israel." *Canadian Jewish Review*, June 11, 1943; also in *Jewish Standard*, June 1943.

"Communists of Canada and Tibor Eckhardt; reply to S. Szöke." *Saturday Night*, January 9, 1943.

"The four freedoms." *Canadian Messenger*, July 1943.

"Hitler's Scandinavian victims." *Scandinavian News*, April 1, 1943.

"In search of Canadian Baptist unity." *Canadian Baptist*, November 15, 1943.

"Nos communistes canadiens." *Relations*, September 1943.

"On putting hand to plough." *Canadian Author and Bookman*, Autumn 1943.

"Our Canadian communists." *Torch*, December 1943.

"Poland's stand has helped allies." *Hamilton Spectator*, May 19, 1943.

"Should post-war immigration into Canada be unrestricted?" *Monetary Times*, July 1, 1943.

The following articles were syndicated by the Writers' War Committee of Canada, 1943:

"Jack the giant killer"
"Tunisian victory"

The following article was syndicated through the Canadian Friends of Poland, 1943:

"Polish literature in Canada."

"The Baptist Federation of Canada." *Maritime Baptist*, December 6, 1944.

"Gatley-Phillip does Poland an injustice." *Saturday Night*, June 24, 1944.

"Independence of Soviet Republics is a myth." *Saturday Night*, March 25, 1944.

"On poetry." *Canadian Poetry Magazine*, September 1944.

"On tone colour." *Canadian Poetry Magazine*, December 1944.

"Adam Mickiewicz, Polish national poet." *Polish Institute of Arts and Sciences in America. Bulletin*, April and July, 1945.

"Communism and Christianity." *Evening Telegram*, May 26, 1945.

"Education in Canada." *Culture*, December 1945.

"Freedom came early in Poland." *Hamilton Spectator*, May 3, 1945.

"Les humanités à notre époque," traduit de Maurice Lebel. *Le Canada français*, septembre et octobre, 1945.

"The humanities in our time." *Canadian School Journal*, April 1945.

"In Memoriam: David Lloyd George." *Canadian Baptist*, April 15, 1945.

"Jewish tribulations under the Soviet régime." *Evening Telegram*, May 17, 1945.

"On imagery." *Canadian Poetry Magazine*, June 1945.

"On rhythm." *Canadian Poetry Magazine*, March 1945.

"On Soviet imperialism." *Evening Telegram*, May 12, 1945.

"On the ethics of controversy." *Evening Telegram*, May 18, 19, and 21, 1945.

"Patterns in narrative verse." *Canadian Poetry Magazine*, December 1945.

"Preface to San Francisco." *Evening Telegram*, April 14, 1945.

"A threat to civil liberties." *Maritime Baptist*, November 28, 1945.

"Three acres of vacation." *School*, June 1945.

"Ukrainian communists in Canada." *America*, December 1, 1945, and December 15, 1945.

"Baptists from sea to sea." *Canadian Baptist*, December 1, 1946.

"Communist morality." *Evening Telegram*, March 25, 1946.

"The crucifixion of Poland." *Evening Telegram*, February 23, 1946.

"The devil's social gospel." *Social Forum*, May 1946.

"Diplomat from Moscow." *Evening Telegram*, March 1, 1946.

"Eclipse of Baltic freedom." *Evening Telegram*, February 16, 1946.

"Franco must go." *Evening Telegram*, March 9, 1946.

"Frelsissólin gengur til vidar í Eystrasaltslöndunum." *Heimskringla*, April 24, 1946.

"History falsified." *Evening Telegram*, November 20, 1946.

"On tempo in verse." *Canadian Poetry Magazine*, March 1946.

"Red threat to labour." *Evening Telegram*, March 16, 1946.

"Spawn of a conspiracy." *Canadian Messenger*, May 1946.

"Tito's red terror." *Evening Telegram*, March 2, 1946.

"The blanket of the dark." *Baltic Review*, 1947.

"Comintern reveals its hand." *Globe and Mail*, October 8, 1947.

"Communists plan destruction." *Globe and Mail*, December 4, 1947.

"The Kremlin organizes Canadian women." *Echoes*, Autumn, 1947.

"Nothing to celebrate in U.S.S.R.'s laws." *Saturday Night*, November 15, 1947.

"Our moral problems as a nation." *Maritime Baptist*, September 3, 1947. Also in *Canadian Baptist*, October 1, 1947.

"Out of own mouth Russia is judged." *Saturday Night*, November 15, 1947.

"Pattern for extermination." *Revue de l'Université d'Ottawa*, janvier-mars 1947.

"Primrose path of liquor legislation." *Canadian Baptist*, January 17, 1947.

"Property rights in Russia doom of human rights." *Saturday Night*, October 18, 1947.

"Social and economic security in the U.S.S.R." *American Economic Security*, January 1947.

"Ukrainian-Canadian literature." *Opinion*, September-October, 1947. Also in *Ukrainian Weekly*, December 1 and 8, 1947.

"Les Ukrainiens au Canada." *Relations*, novembre 1947.

"U.N.R.R.A. accomplice of greatest slave state." *Evening Telegram*, January 2, 1947.

"Arms and torture along Soviet frontier." *Evening Telegram*, June 1, 1948.

"Canadian Baptists and the World Council of Churches." *Maritime Baptist*, February 18, 1948. Also in *Canadian Baptist*, April 15, 1948, and also in *Western Baptist*, March 1948.

"Communism in Canada and the U.S.A." *Canadian Catholic Historical Association. Transactions*. 1948.

"Communists and parliament." *Globe and Mail*, June 3, 1948.

"Communists know what it means." *Evening Telegram*, January 31, 1948.

"Galloping consumption of alcohol." *Canadian Baptist*, May 15, 1948.

"Things that endure." *Acadia Bulletin*, September 1948.

"The Universities of Canada." *Universities Review* (Bristol, England), May 1948.

"Canada in the Moscow press: a year's record." *Financial Post*, September 10, 1949.

"Canada's Communist party." *New Leader*, October 29, 1949.

"Church and university." *Acadia Bulletin*, May, 1949.

"Communists on the Canadian campus are now briefed for their missions." *Saturday Night*, January 18, 1949.

"How much do the Russians know of us?" *Financial Post*, September 10, 1949.

"Nova Scotia suite." *Saturday Night*, February 22, 1949.

"Poems of faith, translated from the Polish language." *Acadia Bulletin*, March 1949.

"Poetry of the New Canadians." *U.C.N.Y.P.U. Program annual*, 1949.

"Religion in Higher Education" (Extracts from a paper read to the Humanities Research Council of Canada, June 10, 1949). *Acadia Bulletin*, November 1949.

"Ukrainian literature in exile." *Opinion*, April 1949.

"The age of frustration." *Acadia Bulletin*, March 1950.

"At the feet of Gamaliel." *Maritime Baptist*, October 11, 1950.

"A ballad of Saint Andrew." *Chronicle-Herald*, November 30, 1950.

"Canada—amalgam of races." *A.Y.P.A. Monthly*, February 1950.

"The Canadian Slav Congress." *Winnipeg Free Press*, March 23, 1950.

"The church and the world." *Maritime Baptist*, August 23, 1950.

"The contents of the arts curriculum." *Acadia Bulletin*, March 1950.

"Greeks mourn their children." *Chronicle-Herald*, May 27, 1950.

"Higher education and the church college." *Maritime Baptist*, January 18, 1950.

"Ilyen hirek érkeznek Amerikába Magyarországról." *Hungaria* (Bad-Worishofen, Germany), September 29, 1950.
"A message of remembrance." *Acadia Bulletin*, November 1950.
"Modern Icelandic poets." *Winnipeg Free Press*, August 26, 1950.
"The New Canadians." *Maritime Baptist*, April 26, 1950.
"A rime of Glooscap." *Dalhousie Review*, October 1950.
"Two Soviet labour documents." *Revue de l'Université d'Ottawa*, octobre-décembre 1950.
"Who are Jehovah's Witnesses?" *Maritime Baptist*, May 10, 1950.
"Bliss Carman." *Sun Life Review*, January 1951.
"Faith and education." *Maritime Baptist*, October 3, 1951.
"Historical stratification in Canadian cultures" (Brussels). *Institut international des civilizations différentes. Compte rendu*, 1951.
"Metaphysics and human freedom." *Acadia Bulletin*, November 1951.
"The preeminent name." *Maritime Baptist*, October 24, 1951.
"Research on Communism." *Australian Church Record*, May 31, 1951.
"The returning." *Chronicle-Herald*, December 24, 1951.
"Seven candles for Acadia." *Financial Times*, July 20, 1951.
"Seven years of Federation." *Maritime Baptist*, December 5, 1951.
"The spirit of Lazarus." *Maritime Baptist*, May 16, 1951.
"Stealing a poet." *Globe and Mail*, April 7, 1951.
"The anatomy of college finance." *Acadia Bulletin*, March 1952.
"I have called you friends." *Maritime Baptist*, October 8, 1952.
"Spanish-American poetry." *Shevchenko Scientific Society. Philological Section. Proceedings*, 1952.
"Reményik, Sándor. Star beneath the water; Write, O Poet!; To the Magyars of Transylvania: poems translated by Watson Kirkconnell." *South Atlantic Quarterly*, January 1952.
"Totalitarian education." *Dalhousie Review*, Summer 1952.
"The Canadian Baptist fellowship." *Canadian Baptist*, March 2, 1953.
"The International Union of Students." *Athenaeum*, October 27, 1953, and November 3, 1953.
"Stephen G. Stephansson and North America." *Lögberg*, August 20, 1953.
"Three rival gospels." Syndicated by the British and Foreign Bible Society. *Canadian Baptist*, November 1, 1953.
"With the understanding also." *Maritime Baptist*, October 7, 1953.
"Aeneas of Lydda." *Maritime Baptist*, September 26, 1954.
"A century of Canadian Baptist history." *Maritime Baptist*, January 20, 1954. Also in *Canadian Baptist*, January 1, 1954.
"A hundred years of school." *Watchman-Warder*, October 13, 1954.
"The Pereyaslav tercentenary." *Svoboda*, July 1, 8, and 15, 1954.
"Some tasks of a federation." *Maritime Baptist*, October 13, 1954.
"Tribute to Marshall Saunders." *Canadian Author and Bookman*, Spring 1954.
"Acadia's governors." *Acadia Bulletin*, April 1955.
"The bells of Chester." *Maritime Baptist*, November 3, 1954.

125

"Canadian scholars." *Acadia Bulletin*, April 1955.
"The epic poetry of Mickiewicz." *Royal Society of Canada. Transactions*, 1955.
"Guarding the heart." *Maritime Baptist*, September 25, 1955.
"Integrity in foreign policy." *Ukrainian Quarterly*, 1955.
"A New Year's prayer." *Canadian Baptist*, January 1, 1955.
"A Scotch Canadian meets Polish." *Dziedzictwo*, May 1955.
"Silas Rand and Glooscap." *Acadia Bulletin*, January 1955.
"Some thirty years ago with C.A.A." *Canadian Author and Bookman*, Winter 1955-56.
"After twenty-five centuries." *Maritime Baptist*, October 17, 1956.
"The Baptist enterprise," an address to the Baptist Federation of Canada, August 27, 1956. *Maritime Baptist*, September 19, 1956.
"Comments on the antiquity of masonry" (Minneapolis). *Bulletin no. 28 of Educational Lodge no. 1002*, December 1, 1956.
"Foreword on request." *Canadian Poetry Magazine*, Autumn 1956.
"The martyrdom of Hungary." *Athenaeum*, November 9, 1956.
"The phoenix of our valley of the west" (poem). *Acadia Bulletin*, April 1956.
"Thirty-six years of constitutions." *Canadian Author and Bookman*, Winter 1956.
"Higher education in Nova Scotia," a data paper. *Acadia Bulletin*, April 1957.
"Music from the sidelines." *Canadian Music Journal*, Summer 1957.
"The place of understanding," an address at an S.C.M. Service, September 29, 1957. *Maritime Baptist*, October 23, 1957.
Tollas, Tibor. Poems translated from the Magyar by Watson Kirkconnell. *Nemzetör*, April 1957.
"Abraham Lincoln." *Acadia School of Theology Bulletin*, March 1958.
"Acadia alumni as professors, a study." *Acadia Bulletin*, January 1958.
"Baptist highlights of the past hundred years." *Canadian Baptist*, July 1958.
"The Canadian Arts Council." *Canadian Author and Bookman*, Summer 1958.
"Maritime university problems." *Atlantic Advocate*, May 1958.
"Royal commission on copyright—a review." *Canadian Author and Bookman*, Autumn 1958.
"Soviet law." *New Leader*, June 2, 1958.
"A text from Numbers." *Maritime Baptist*, March 5, 1958.
"This word 'Ecumenical'." *Maritime Baptist*, February 19, 1958.
"What, when, where, why, and how of the Canadian Conference of the Arts." *Canadian Author and Bookman*, Summer 1958.
"Breaking through language curtains." *Educational Record*, April-June 1959.
"Magyar revolutionary poets." *Athenaeum*, October 30, 1959.

"Ukrainian language and literature." *Globe and Mail*, November 26, 1959.

"At the back of the north wind." *Acadian*, May 5, 1960.

"The Caucasian chalk circle." *Athenaeum*, November 19, 1960.

"The hills of remembrance." *Educational Record*, October-December, 1960.

"The reign of King Malcolm" (an address by President Kirkconnell at a testimonial dinner in honour of Dr. Malcolm Elliott, December 1, 1959). *Acadia Bulletin*, February 1960.

"The Ides of March and the Kalends of November." *Fáklyaláng*, March 1961.

"Man's unconquerable soul." *Hungarian Week Book*, 1961.

"The miracle of Taras Shevchenko." *Winnipeg Free Press*, July 7, 1961.

"Our university's future." *Maritime Baptist*, February 22, 1961.

"The parish primeval." *Acadian*, April 20, 1961.

"Problems of the future, an assembly talk," January 16, 1961. *Acadia Bulletin*, April 1961.

"Religion in Soviet Russia." *Maritime Baptist*, December 13, 1961.

"The Shevchenko centenary." *Ukrainian Quarterly*, Spring 1961.

"Ukrayinska literatura v Kanadi." *Kanadyskyj Farmer*, February 1961; also in *Ukrayinskyj Holos*, February 1961; also in *Novy Shlyakh*, February 1961.

"Acadia extended." *Chronicle-Herald*. Industrial review and forecast, 1962.

"Education and private enterprise, an address." *Industrial Canada*, July 1962.

"Foreign language publications in Canada." *Canadian Library Association. Proceedings*, 1962.

"Hat évvel ezelött." *Nemzetör*, October 15, 1962.

"A Janus-look at Acadia." *Acadia Bulletin*, January 1963.

"Ohlyad Ukrainskykh v Kanadi Za 1961 rik." *Canadian Farmer*, October 1, 1962.

"The Polish epic." *Illustrowany Kalendarz Czasu*, 1962.

"Acadia University; rapid expansion biggest problem." *Mail-Star*, January 8, 1963.

"The bicentennial twins." *Maritime Baptist*, October 2, 1963.

"Four decades of Icelandic poetry in Canada, 1922-1962." *Icelandic-Canadian*, Winter 1963.

"A possession forever." *Icelandic-Canadian*, September 1963.

"There were giants in those days, a tribute to Dr. G. B. Cutten." *Acadia Bulletin*, January 1963.

"Le Témoignage des oies sauvages." *Revue de l'Université Laval*, septembre 1963.

"The way of the translator." *Polish Review*, Summer 1963.

"Gloria victis." *Fáklyaláng*, October 1964.

"The highway of knowledge, convocation address," August 14, 1964. *Acadia Bulletin*, October 1964.
"A presidential valedictory." *Acadia Bulletin*, April 1964.
"A president's farewell." *Athenaeum*, April 3, 1964.
"Thingvellir." *Icelandic-Canadian*, April 1964.
"Vdyachne sertse" (tr. by C. Ewach). *Ukrainian Voice*, April 15, 1964.
"The Christian layman," an address delivered on Baptist Men's Sunday, October 17, 1965, in the Wolfville Baptist Church. *Atlantic Baptist*, November 15, 1965.
"The Shevchenko monument in Washington." *Svoboda*, May 29, 1965.
Ukrainian translations by O. Hay-Holowka of three poems by Watson Kirkconnell. *Nowi Dni*, December 1965.
"The Byron of St. Petersburg." *Winnipeg Free Press*, March 5, 1966.
"Drazha dies a martyr." *Glas Kanadskykh Srba*, July 14, 1966. Also a translation of the same poem into Serb by Matej Matejic, same paper, July 28, 1967.
"Edda and Saga abroad." *Lögberg-Heimskringla*, annual literary supplement, February 1966.
"From wells of memory." *Athenaeum*, March 10, 1967.
"Islenzkt skald: Kanada." *Lesbók Morgunbladsins*, June 18, 1967.
"The Loyalists of Nova Scotia." *Loyalist Gazette*, Autumn 1969.
"Milton: a tercentenary stock-taking." *Dalhousie Review*, Winter 1969/ 70.
"Many voices and one chorus." *German Canadian Business Review*, Fall 1970.
"Policy post-mortem." *Public Affairs*, Autumn 1971.
"The first migratory bird." *Icelandic-Canadian*, Spring 1972.

(9) Works completed but unpublished, 1974

A psalter for Everyman: a verse translation of the Book of Psalms (MS. 291 pages).
The Hungarian Helicon (MS. 1180 pages).
Climbing a Green tree and some other branches (MS. 100 pages).

(10) Articles about Watson Kirkconnell

King, Amabel. Editorial. *Canadian Poetry Magazine*, June 1944.
Biographical note. *Public Affairs*, Autumn 1951.
Biographical note. *Canadian Author and Bookman*, Spring 1958.
"Author, poet, and university president." *Canadian Library*, May 1962.
Kirkconnell, James W. "Watson Kirkconnell: a scholarly volcano." *Canadian Author and Bookman*, Winter 1963.
Thompson, M. "Poet and polymath; review article." *Canadian Literature*, Autumn, 1968.